No More Excuses

Michael A. Stevens

CREATION
H O U S E
A STRANG COMPANY

No More Excuses by Michael A. Stevens
Published by Creation House
A Strang Company
600 Rinehart Road
Lake Mary, Florida 32746
www.creationhouse.com

Scripture quotations marked NLT are from the Holy Bible, New Living Translation, copyright © 1996. Used by permission of Tyndale House Publishers, Inc., Wheaton, IL 60189. All rights reserved.

Scripture quotations marked NKJV are from the New King James Version of the Bible. Copyright © 1979, 1980, 1982 by Thomas Nelson, Inc., publishers. Used by permission.

Scripture quotations marked NIV are from the Holy Bible, New International Version of the Bible. Copyright © 1973, 1978, 1984, International Bible Society. Used by permission.

Cover design by Jerry Pomales

Library of Congress Control Number: 2008929195
International Standard Book Number: 978-1-59979-391-7

First Edition

08 09 10 11 12 — 987654321
Printed in the United States of America

CONTENTS

DEDICATION

This book is dedicated to my father,
Rudolph Stevens—who took me to church!
This book is also dedicated to Michael
and Matthew, my two sons—
whom I now take to church!

ACKNOWLEDGEMENTS

I EXPRESS A GREAT appreciation to the many men of God who dared to make a difference by becoming an authority on this much-needed subject matter—Dr. Jawanza Kunjufu, David Murrow, the late Dr. Edward Cole, Harry Jackson, Bishop Charles E. Blake, Bishop Vaughn McLaughlin, Bishop Donald Hilliard, Bishop Phillip Davis, Dr. Patrick Wooden, Dr. Wellington Boone, and my pastor and spiritual father, Dr. Otis Lockett.

To Julia Nelson, Allen Quain, Stephen Strang and the staff of both the University City Church and Michael A. Stevens International Ministries. Thanks for the untiring and unwavering commitment and consistency toward building God's kingdom—in the local community and the global marketplace at large. Finally, many thanks to my wife, Sharon, and our graceful and loving children—Michael, Matthew, and Charisma.

Much love…much love!

PREFACE

T his Sunday, more than six million wives will attend church faithfully—without their husbands. Thousands of African-American children will attend Sunday schools and children's church while Daddy watches the game or sleeps in. No wonder 90 percent of those same little boys will leave the church by their teens or early twenties. Many will never return.

This book is written for those of us who want them back. It is for the bewildered mothers who took their sons to church and now search for them in vain on Sunday mornings. It is for the girlfriend or fiancée who waits patiently for that man to get to church at least once so he can make her a wife. It is for the wife who has run out of excuses for her husband's absences and for the pastors and leaders who have thrown up their hands in frustration instead of praise.

Finally, this book is written for the black man himself; a man once considered the invincible one, but now—the invisible one. This is a man whose ancestors stood against adversity with fearless faith and determination and led their families with pride. Now he is missing from the foyers and fellowship halls of the church. Where is he? What will it take to bring him home?

> He won over the hearts of all the men of Judah as
> though they were one man.
>
> —2 Samuel 19:14, niv

FOREWORD

P ASTOR MICHAEL A. Stevens is a young man who is passionate about reaching the men of our generation especially among the African-American community. I greatly appreciate his passion for combating the shortage of men in our church. His conviction and competence are greatly evident in this ministry of teaching and preaching among the body of Christ.

If there has ever been a time or a need for a book like this, it is now! With high school dropouts, the down-low epidemic, and single-parent homes at an all-time high, *No More Excuses* is a practical book that deals with the challenges and issues men face today. Pastor Stevens tackles each subject with biblical accuracy, divine authority, and a God-given anointing.

It is time that men take their rightful place in the home, in society, and the church. It is even a greater blessing that my dear friend Pastor Stevens has taken on the challenge of helping men achieve this ever-important goal.

—Bishop Charles Edward Blake
Presiding Bishop, Church of God in Christ

INTRODUCTION

Sunday morning arrived, like so many before, with a mix of sunlight and chirping birds outside my bedroom window and a warm greeting from my tiny son, lying beside my wife and me. My wife rose quickly, announcing her plan to jump in the shower and get ready for Sunday school at the Baptist church, not far from our house in suburban Chicago, that she and our two children attend.

As for me, in what has become my ritual nowadays, I turned over and pulled the covers up around my head. Soon I overheard my nine-year-old daughter's familiar question: "Mommy, is Daddy going to church with us?"

"No-o-o-o," my wife replied. After months of my failure to accompany them, she has abandoned the excuse that "Daddy has a lot of work to do."

Sunday mornings used to mean something special to me. But I now face them with dread, with a bittersweet sorrow that tugs at my heart and a headache-inducing tension that makes me reach for the Advil. I am torn between my desire to play hooky from church and my Pentecostal indoctrination that Sunday is the Lord's day, a day of worship when real men are supposed to lead their families into the house of God.

> Yet I now feel disconnected. I am disconnected.
> Not necessarily from God, but from the church.
> —John W. Fountain[1]

———•———

In the dead of night, a man and his wife lift their children from their pallets on the floor and steal silently into the woods. They walk for half an hour in the dark until they reach the worship service. They are slaves at the turn of the nineteenth century, and they are risking their lives to be at church.

Now look out over a sanctuary in a typical African-American church today. It's Sunday morning and what do you see? You will see far more women than men. A grandfather sings in the choir. A few little boys cling to their mothers' skirts. But mostly there are women. These are women that have jobs and children, but they are in church without their husbands, brothers, and fathers. Most of their sons will stop coming when they are old enough to be home by themselves.

From the wreckage of Ground Zero after September 11, 2001, Bill Hybels proclaimed, "The church is the hope of the world and its future rests primarily in the hands of its leaders."[2] I agree with him. In an age of increasing danger and uncertainty, the church still holds the answer. Faced with our own wreckage and ruin, I believe the hope of the black community still lies in the church as well.

God is a God of order. The African-American man still needs the church, and the African-American family still needs its man. God has anointed the man to serve his family as prophet, priest, protector, and provider. Nothing can ever replace him. When he is in his place doing his job, everything else falls in line.

Author and community activist Dr. Jawanza Kunjufu discussed the topic of his well-known book, *Adam, Where Are You? Why Most Black Men Don't Go to Church*, in April 2006. He observed that when a child is saved and attends church, it has little effect on the rest of the family. When a wife or mother is saved, it has a greater effect; her children go with her while they are young, and perhaps a sister or a cousin as well. Yet when a man gets saved, overwhelmingly the rest of the family will follow him to church and to salvation.[3]

This reality is why I wrote this book. The hope for the multitude of social problems we face in the African-American community is wrapped up in the black man's return to his church. I want to explore how we, as black men, went from risking our lives to worship God to abandoning His church and too often our families as well. I will expose many negative factors that have contributed to this destructive trend. These are not things that most of us are comfortable discussing, but I feel strongly that they need to be brought into the light.

I also want to share what we can do about it. God has blessed me with a church full of young, ambitious, masculine black men. These are men who are learning to be leaders in their homes, on their jobs, and in their communities. I believe God has given me wisdom to understand some of these deeper needs and respond to them in a biblical way.

I want to share that understanding with my fellow pastors and church leaders, as well as with the multitudes of believing wives, mothers, and sisters who are waiting for their black men to come home. I know that the words on these pages will bear witness with the hearts of men who read this book, and will call them back to their places. I believe that together we can see broken men healed and restored.

FROM INVINCIBLE TO INVISIBLE

The Journey of Today's Black Man

*I am one of the most irresponsible beings that ever lived.
Irresponsibility is part of my invisibility; any way you face it,
it is a denial. But to whom can I be responsible, and
why should I be, when you refuse to see me?[1]*

—RALPH ELLISON'S *INVISIBLE MAN*

WHILE I DON'T often feel like I identify with Ellison's protagonist, I did have one of those moments not too long ago. I was sitting in first class on a flight from Dallas to Washington, DC, waiting for the plane to take off. I needed some information about my connection, and so I made several vain attempts to get the flight attendant's attention. I made a conscious effort not to focus on the fact that I was the only black in first class, and that she was white.

"Excuse me, Miss," I queried politely, two, three, and four times. She continued serving other passengers. Understanding her busyness and focus on the other passengers, it however became undoubtedly clear that I was and would be for the next few agonizing moments invisible to her. Interestingly at the same time, the gentleman next to me nudged me and asked, "Are you invisible, or what?"

Before that plane landed, I had begun this book.

The Journey of the Black Man

Where did today's African-American man come from? Of course one of our problems is that we can't be completely sure. None of us can name our ancestors past a certain generation. Were they with the group of African slaves that arrived in Jamestown on that Dutch ship in 1619? Or did they come ten, fifty, or one hundred years later? What language did they speak? To which tribe did they belong? There is simply no way to know.

We do know, of course, that most of our ancestors came from somewhere in Africa. Were they descendants of the ancient empire of Mali that supplied gold to the entire world? Maybe they came from the kingdom of Benin with its massive bronze plaques detailing its four hundred-year history. Perhaps, reaching back thousands of years further, they hailed from the realm of the ancient pharaohs or the Cushites that the Bible tells us were feared far and wide:

> But the time will come when the LORD Almighty will receive gifts from this land [Ethiopia, Cush] divided by rivers, from this tall, smooth-skinned people, who are feared far and wide for their conquests and destruction. They will bring the gifts to the LORD Almighty in Jerusalem, the place where his name dwells.
>
> —Isaiah 18:7, NLT

Again, we simply don't know.

We do know, however, that the first Africans in the Americas were purchased by Spanish colonialists from Arab slave traders who had conquered northern Africa in the seventh century. We know the transatlantic slave trade continued to what is now the United States for more than 250 years. We know that during this time, even more of our brothers and sisters were marched across the Sahara to slavery in the Middle East. Their names, too, are forgotten.

And what is our legacy since our ancestors arrived on these shores? Is our story one solely of oppression, abuse, and grief? Or is it also one of longsuffering, endurance, and triumph? In a way, I believe we are still deciding the answer.

There is no doubt that our history in the United States is stained with mourning: forced toil, beatings, and families ripped apart by sale or death. Yet how did our people respond to these unimaginable trials? Today, we observe ethnic and religious clashes that leave children and grandmothers dead. To whom did our ancestors cry out for deliverance?

I believe the story of African-Americans is one of survival and triumph. I confess that I wish I knew more about my African heritage. It would be nice to know if I came from Mali or Ghana or Songhai. It would be great to know if my ancestors were kings or serfs. But not knowing has not stopped me from fulfilling God's destiny for my life.

I do believe that part of reclaiming our destiny is reclaiming our history. Whether you see yourself in the ancient Cushites of Isaiah 18 or reach back just a few hundred years, the legacy of our ancestors is worthy of our pride. From the earliest days of the United States, free blacks, though few in number, overcame racism and achieved remarkable things. After emancipation, black Americans went from a 1 percent literacy rate to more than 80 percent literate in less than a generation.

During the first half of the twentieth century, black unemployment was no higher than white unemployment, and often it was lower. African-American men worked hard. They readily took two or three jobs to make sure their wives and children had enough to eat. They knew they had to face racism and the poorer educational opportunities afforded to them, but they also knew they had to do what they had to do to be husbands and fathers.

The majority of black men in those days agreed with Booker T. Washington when he said, "We should not permit our grievances to overshadow our opportunities."[2] In 1960, more than 70 percent of black American babies were born to homes headed by their fathers. Poverty, racism, and lack of educational resources were far worse than they are today, yet black men were, for the most part, in their place.

The Disappearing Black Man

How different things are today. Everywhere we look, the black man is disappearing. He is disappearing from the ranks of high school graduates: black males have a low graduation rate among the ethnic groups in America. He is disappearing from the workforce, with the highest unemployment rate of any demographic category, nearly twice that of whites and Hispanics.

He is even disappearing from free society. A sadly high

proportion of young African-American adult males are incarcerated, compared to very low proportions of Hispanic men or white men near the same age group. He is disappearing fast: the number of black men in prison is significantly higher than what it was twenty years ago.

In short, the African-American man has become nearly invisible.

Empty altars

Now let us look at what every black woman knows is the heart of the matter: how many of these black men are actually "marriageable"? Where are the black husbands?

According to the 2000 Census:

- nationwide, there are only 7 single black men for every 10 single black women.[3] (There are approximately 10.8 million black men over the age of eighteen, compared to 13.5 million black women. There are 5.7 mil unmarried black men and 8.1 million unmarried black women.);
- 800,000 of the black men are incarcerated;
- approximately 1,000,000 black men are living as homosexual or on the down-low;
- 42.4 percent of black women have never been married, more than double the percentage in 1950[4];
- black men were only 63 percent as likely as white men to marry for the first time between ages 25 and 29.[5]

What we have now is a population of marriageable black men (not taking into account education and employment) that is just a fraction of the population of black women who need husbands. As the black man disappears from marriage, he disappears from the home. As I wrote about in my first book, *Straight Up: The Church's Official Response to the Epidemic of Down-Low Living*, more than 70 percent of black children are now born to unmarried mothers.[6] Far too many black men have succumbed to the demonic influence of homosexuality. They are either openly gay or living on the "down-low," (Approximately 25 percent of African-American men who have sex with other men consider themselves heterosexual.)

Thanks to this, AIDS is not only the leading cause of death for black men aged 18–44, but the leading cause of death for black women in that age group as well. All but a tiny fraction of those women got AIDS from having sex with a man who also has sex with men. According to the Centers for Disease Control, about a third of urban black homosexuals are HIV positive. Now, 70 percent of all new HIV cases are black women, representing an infection rate twenty times the rate of white women in America.

What happened? How did we survive slavery to complain that we can't catch a break on the job? How did we fight our way to the front of the bus only to fail to graduate from high school? Surely our grandfathers did not win honors in the military so that our young men today languish in gangs and jails. God did not bring our ancestors through near-starvation so we could die of sexually transmitted diseases (STDs).

I believe that there is no question that the decline of the African-American male is directly correlated to his exodus from the church. We have forgotten that it was God all along who sustained us through the Middle Passage, the centuries of slavery, Jim Crow laws, and segregation. It was God who delivered us, and as we shall see later, His church was a central part of His plan of deliverance.

As James 1:13–15 reminds us, "Let no one say when he is tempted, 'I am tempted by God'; for God cannot be tempted by evil, nor does He Himself tempt anyone. But each one is tempted when he is drawn away by his own desires and enticed. Then, when desire has conceived, it gives birth to sin; and sin, when it is full-grown, brings forth death." This is true for all people, regardless of race or gender. Black men have enough to deal with in this life without reaping death and destruction from their own sin.

The apostle Paul builds on Jesus' teaching in Romans 5:18–19, "Therefore, as through one man's offense judgment came to all men, resulting in condemnation, even so through one Man's righteous act the free gift came to all men, resulting in justification of life. For as by one man's disobedience many were made sinners, so also by one Man's obedience many will be made righteous" (NKJV). Black men need to know that their hope is the power of Jesus' forgiveness and the grace He offers toward repentance.

On blogs and street corners and in barbershops and town hall meetings, many black men are voicing concerns and complaints with today's church and its leadership. Some men feel that the church doesn't help them at all; they see it as a

Sunday morning moneymaking scheme. Others are bored with endless services or disgusted by hypocrisy. A segment of the educated black men who have left the church complain that it has become irrelevant to the black community in the twenty-first century.

In my observation there are also a number of African-American males who simply cannot cope with the idea of submitting to a male moral authority figure. The lack of a father in the home has filled them with resentment against all male leadership, so they "stumble in noonday as in twilight" (Isa. 59:10), rather than take counsel from someone who could guide and encourage them. Whatever the reasons these men give, the net result has not been good. I wonder how many of them could honestly say they are better off for having abandoned the church.

Dr. Robert Franklin, professor of social ethics at Emory University's Candler School of Theology observes, "The problem isn't the church. The problem is with man's own spiritual journey and identity. It's not exactly clear when the schism began. In that ancient garden? The migration to the inner city? Or in more recent years? What seems certain, however, is the impact of the mass migration of Americans to urban areas."[7] Dr. Kunjufu adds, "In a more rural environment there was a closer percentage of men and women in church and more youth…as more of us became urbanized, fewer men attended and mothers didn't require their sons to attend."[8]

Despite these trends, I believe the church still holds the answer to the black man's problems. But first I want to take a close look at those problems, which find their root all the way back in the Garden. As we will see, at their core, the problems of today's African-American men are no more than the problems of man himself.

2

IN THE BEGINNING

God's Plan for Adam and What Went Wrong

The church must be reminded that it is not the master or the servant of the state, but rather the conscience of the state. It must be the guide and the critic of the state, and never its tool. If the church does not recapture its prophetic zeal, it will become an irrelevant social club without moral or spiritual authority.

—DR. MARTIN LUTHER KING, JR[1]

FOR MORE THAN forty years, people have been talking and writing about the African-American family and how it came to be in its current condition. I am certainly not the first to observe that the vast majority of problems our families are facing can be traced to the African-American man. Black women, after all, are becoming college graduates in record numbers. They are breaking through racial barriers and attaining professional positions that were closed to them just two generations ago. But where is the black American man?

In this chapter, I want to examine how the present day condition of the black American man has its root in the Garden of Eden, at the dawn of Creation itself. It is easy to talk about African-American males as peculiar or unique specimens of certain behavior. I think, upon further examination, that we will find their problems the problems of all mankind since the Fall. In some ways those problems may seem distilled or concentrated, but their roots are common to all.

At one time, when racism was greater, poverty was worse and educational opportunities were far scarcer, black men were the backbone of their churches, families, and communities. They dressed in their Sunday best with pride to come to the one place where they found dignity and respect in a harsh world. Each man had his wife and children with him.

What happened?

CREATED FOR DOMINION

The first two chapters of Genesis give us a picture of God's original intentions for His creation. They lay a foundation for how we are to understand the world in which we live. In Genesis 1, we see God as a Being of infinite creative ability, painting a breathtaking landscape on an empty void as He speaks the universe into existence.

This incomprehensible Creator makes mankind in His image and gives him dominion and rule over everything in the Earth. Unlike today, when we tremble at the approach of a wild animal, Adam could speak to them with authority. When meditating on that, I sometimes cannot help but think of Tarzan communicating with the apes in the jungle. Yet I realize it was much more profound than that. Adam didn't merely live among the animals; he ruled them as their undisputed lord.

Adam had everything he would ever need in the Garden. He lacked for nothing. And still in verse 28 we see that, "God blessed them, and God said to them, 'Be fruitful and multiply; fill the earth and subdue it; have dominion over the fish of the sea, over the birds of the air, and over every living thing that moves on the earth.'" God had met all of Adam's physical needs, and yet He still had an important task for him to accomplish. We understand that when God "blessed" Adam and his wife, He empowered them to prosper and fill the Earth with His glory.

Adam's authority was part of creative order. His leadership ability came from his innermost nature. He didn't have to learn how to subdue the Earth; he merely spoke to the living things on the Earth and they did his bidding. He was the model of invincibility. Who could stand against Adam's mighty voice? Who could stand against the man God Himself had set over the Earth to rule it and subdue it?

CREATED FOR WORSHIP

Thus the heavens and the earth, and all the host of them, were finished. And on the seventh day God ended His work which He had done, and He rested on the seventh day from all His work which He had done. Then God blessed the seventh day and sanctified it, because in it He rested from all His work which God had created and made. This is the history of the heavens and the earth when they were created, in the day that the LORD God made the earth and the heavens, before any plant of the field was in the earth and before any herb of the field had grown. For the LORD God had not caused it to rain on the earth, and there was no man to till the ground; but a mist went up from the earth and watered the whole face of the ground. And the LORD God formed man of the dust of the ground, and breathed into his nostrils the breath of life; and man became a living being.

—Genesis 2:1–7

In this passage, God gives us insight into a completely unique window of time. The act of creation was complete. Plants were created, but existed only as seeds in the soil. The Earth was complete, but all was motionless. God formed Adam from the dust of the Earth, but He had not yet given Adam the breath of life. He existed as a motionless mannequin, awaiting the touch of His Creator.

We have all likely sung the words from Psalm 150:6 that declare: "Let everything that has breath praise the Lord." We know from this passage that God created man to work in the garden, and interestingly enough the Hebrew words for worship and work in this case come from the same root: *abbas.*

All of creation was in a state of suspended animation, ready to burst into bloom. The soil waited for rain to call forth life from countless seeds and the empty shell of the first man waited for breath so he could worship his Creator.

We see here that Adam's first duty was to worship. That is still the case today. The first obligation of every man of any color is to worship. This is not just singing and traditional worship, of course. It is the dedication of every act, every breath, and every effort to the glory of God. Yet too many men are still in state of suspended animation. They are still empty shells and lifeless mannequins because they refuse to worship their Creator.

CREATED FOR HIS WOMAN

It is incredible to ponder that Adam in all his abundance, with the God of the universe as his Companion, was in any way incomplete. Yet God said it was so:

> And the Lord God said, "It is not good that man should be alone; I will make him a helper comparable to him." Out of the ground the Lord God formed every beast of the field and every bird of the air, and brought them to Adam to see what he would call them. And whatever Adam called each living creature that was its name. So Adam gave names to all cattle, to the birds of the air, and to every beast of the field. But for Adam there was not found a helper comparable to him. And the Lord God caused a deep sleep to fall on Adam, and he slept; and He took one of his ribs, and closed up the flesh in its place. Then the rib which the Lord God had taken from man He made into a woman, and He brought her to the man. And Adam said: "This is now bone of my bones and flesh of my flesh; She shall be called Woman, because she was taken out

of Man." Therefore a man shall leave his father and mother and be joined to his wife, and they shall become one flesh. And they were both naked, the man and his wife, and were not ashamed.

—Genesis 2:18–25

God made it clear from the very beginning that Adam could not fulfill His will without his woman at his side. This first perfect union, brought together by God Himself, was full of the strength of purity and the joy of innocence. The man and his wife were naked and not ashamed. They had no dark secrets to tell each other, no terrible past to keep concealed. Adam, who had the whole world for his playground, and all the animals for his sport, was at last complete. Far from a burden or an obligation, Adam's wife was his crowning reward, his greatest gift from his Creator.

WHAT HAPPENED?

So what happened to the original invincible man? How did he lose the best set-up imaginable? I want to sidestep some of the age-old theological arguments surrounding Genesis 3, and focus on a few relevant points. Adam didn't wake up that morning looking for trouble. He didn't seek out the serpent and try to think of a way to ruin his life. At the heart of the story of the fall of the human race is an irresponsible man.

At first glance the first six verses of Genesis 3 seem focused on Adam's wife (not yet named, it is worth noting). She and the serpent are having a conversation, and then we are told in verse 6: "So when the woman saw that the tree was good for food, that it was pleasant to the eyes, and a tree desirable to make one wise, she took of its fruit and ate. She also gave to her husband with her, and he ate."

Adam is completely absent in the first five verses of this crucial chapter, and his role in verse six is strictly passive. The wife to whom he was supposed to be joined was dealing with the serpent alone. How many women today are dealing with the serpents in their lives alone, because their men are nowhere to be found?

Once the woman had been deceived, rather than correct the situation, Adam followed her into sin. We know from then on the innocence of their nakedness was destroyed, and they hid themselves from their own Creator.

"Then the Lord God called to Adam and said to him, 'Where are you?'" (v. 9). It should be obvious to us that God knew where Adam was. He was asking Adam if *he* knew where he was. Thousands of years later, there are countless men who still do not know where they are. The Lord God is still calling to them.

Adam's response to the Lord's confrontation over his disobedience might also sound familiar: "Then the man said, 'The woman whom You gave to be with me, she gave me of the tree, and I ate'" (v. 12). Adam was physically present before the Lord, but he had given up all that authority he previously commanded. "The woman—it was the woman's fault," he answered.

The rest of the curse we know well. The serpent lost his legs, his ability to speak, and was forced to crawl on his belly in the dust. To this day most of us can identify with the enmity put between the woman's offspring and snakes. Women were saddled with pain in childbirth, and men were forced to toil for food instead of tending a garden in joy.

The most important thing to remember about this well-known story is this: Adam didn't fail because he wasn't strong enough. He didn't fail because he wasn't smart enough, didn't have the right background or qualifications. He failed because he ran away. He failed because he hid. He failed because he chose to be invisible.

ADAM AND HIS WORSHIP, HIS WORK, AND HIS WOMAN TODAY

I believe that there are segments of the black community today that magnify the tragic repercussion of Adam's original sin. How many African-American men are walking around as mere shells of themselves, because they have not yet connected with their Creator in worship? How many toil by the sweat of their brow when their Creator is calling them to till His garden with joy? How many are hiding themselves in fraternities or gangs while their Creator calls, "Adam, where are you?"

The lost black man might seek comfort in liquor and promiscuity or in worldly success and wealth. He has no clue who he is or where he is. All around him, black women are graduating from college, advancing in the workplace and leaving him behind. He is not just taking a backseat to women in his professional life. According to the Barna Research Group, women are more likely to attend church, Sunday school classes, and small groups than men. Women pray and read their Bibles more often than men. Sixty-eight percent of women describe themselves as deeply spiritual versus only 55 percent of men.[2]

So this lost man probably grew up seeing church as a "woman" thing. Yet chances are from the time he was a little boy, if something went wrong, there was a woman to intervene and make it right. Who will he blame when things go wrong in his adult life? Will he, like Adam, say it was some woman's fault?

This does not have to be our story. Our legacy of greatness is born out of adversity. As I will discuss in more detail later, our ancestors worshiped God faithfully under the threat of death. Yet today, with access to freedom and opportunity that our forefathers could only dream of, we seem to have more bitterness and irreverence hindering our worship than ever before.

As a pastor, I have noticed that some of the most accomplished men are the most humble, but those who have hardly developed any skills are the ones that won't listen to anyone. I have seen people wait until they are about to lose their houses to come asking for help, when they should have come for financial counseling three months earlier. Our grandparents cleaned homes and worked long hours to make sure our parents had a place to live. Today, we have families evicted because they can't live without cable and designer clothes.

Bill Cosby offended many when he pointed out the obvious: immigrants from Africa and the Caribbean who are every bit as black as any African-American were risking their lives to come to America and often making better use of the opportunities available. While that doesn't mean that racism is not still a problem, it clearly demonstrates that it is not an *insur-mountable* problem. Immigrants come, value education, and see opportunity, while many others see only obstacles.

I believe the change will come when men begin to see what Adam once knew. Work is not toiling with a bad attitude for a paycheck that won't cover half your bills. Work is the worship you owe your Creator. If you wouldn't sing a song to God with a sour expression on your face, you shouldn't do your job that way. As I've already said, worship is offering every part of your life to God. You can't separate worship from how you handle your responsibilities to your family. A man's failure to his woman or his kids is wrapped up in his failure to worship his God. We can see that the same thing that hindered Adam in the Garden hinders men today. Yet God has given us hope. In the chapters that follow we will learn how this hope can be realized in our generation.

3

FATHERLESS FATHERS

The Wounded Generation

Dad is Destiny![1]

I WILL NEVER FORGET the chill in the air that fall evening when the little boy approached me. No more than seven years old, he shuffled past the rusty sliding board to where I was standing, next to what had once been a swing set. His eyes met mine with excitement and he asked, "Are you my daddy?"

My heart sank. I was not anyone's father back then. I was working at the Boys and Girls Club as a young man, mentoring countless children like this one—children who were searching for Daddy. Years later, that boy's question still reverberates in my memory.

What happens when a man who has never known his father has a child himself? We see the answer to this question in far too many families today: young men who have never known the discipline of a father's presence or the security of his love repeating the cycle of neglect with their own. Two or even three generations of children are now reaping the curses that God warned us about:

> And he will turn the hearts of the fathers to the children, and the hearts of the children to their fathers, lest I come and strike the earth with a curse.

—Malachi 4:6

Yet God the heavenly Father is ready to bless. He is more than able to break the curses of fatherlessness that have plagued the black community in particular. I have found, however, that these curses cannot be broken if we insist on making excuses or denying their existence.

"DAD IS DESTINY"

The cover of *Time Magazine* on Father's Day 2006 read simply, "Dad Is Destiny." Between the covers were studies and statistics confirming the crucial role of the biological father in the lives of his children. Summing up the conclusions of many, educational authors Jeanne Machado and Helen Meyer-Botnarescue state, "More than virtually any other factor a biological father's presence in the family will determine a child's success and happiness."[2]

Eleven years earlier in February 1995, *US News and World Report* declared, "The absence of fathers is linked to most social nightmares from boys with guns to girls with babies."[3]

The nightmare of fatherlessness doesn't stop there. Our relationship with our heavenly Father will be heavily influenced by our relationship with our earthly father. It is much easier to understand the nature of God as a faithful provider who lovingly disciplines His children if you have seen those qualities modeled by your own father at home. If you have not, trusting God often becomes a much more difficult task.

A good father sets you up for success in every area of life. Chances are if your relationship with your father is strong, it will be easier for you to submit to spiritual authority in your church and trust your heavenly Father to take care of your needs. If your dad was an absentee, you may deal a lot more with subtle rebellion issues or lack of faith. This problem is compounded by the lack of true spiritual fathering in many churches.

I believe one of the reasons that so many Christians who consider themselves spiritual run from instructor to instructor and church to church is that they have weak or unhealed relationships with their natural fathers. These Christians struggle to submit to God and His ordained authority as if they are trying to paddle a boat upstream.

> It is sown a natural body, it is raised a spiritual body. There is a natural body, and there is a spiritual body. And so it is written, "The first man Adam became a living being." The last Adam became a life-giving spirit. However, the spiritual is not first, but the natural, and afterward the spiritual.
> —1 Corinthians 15:44–46

God has ordained that we should learn principles first in the natural realm and then in the spiritual. When there is a problem in the natural realm, we will almost always see a corresponding problem spiritually. What, then, can we do about it?

THE FATHER'S PRESENCE

As long as we make excuses for the state of our families, we will never be able to break the curse of fatherlessness. It might seem compassionate to downplay the importance of a father to those whose father has abandoned them. Yet that approach merely puts a Band-aid on a deep wound that must been cleaned, sutured, and healed.

The biological father's presence in the home and active role in the lives of his children is of irreplaceable importance. Author and psychologist Dr. James Dobson asserts that Dad has to be a positive part of a child's life between eighteen months and five years of age, or the child's self-esteem, confidence, and development is permanently affected.[4] The best possible situation for children in general and black children in particular seems to be one in which a married mother and father attend church regularly with their children. Studies directly link a family's church attendance to better behavior and a more positive outlook on life among African-American children: "[Church attendance] is associated with substantial differences in the behavior of [black male youths from poverty-stricken inner-city neighborhoods] and thus in their chances to 'escape' from inner city poverty. It affects allocation of time, school-going, work activity and the frequency of socially deviant activity."[5]

Further findings confirm "the power of religious belief and practice in encouraging a spirit of optimism among socially at-risk but advancing children....within this group, the highest concentration of pessimists is found among students with the lowest attendance at church. Those who attend church weekly or more frequently, on the other hand, exhibit the following profiles:

- They are more optimistic about their futures.
- They have better relationships with their parents.
- They are more likely to dismiss racism as an obstacle to reaching their goals.
- They are more likely to have serious and realistic goals for their futures.
- They are more likely to see themselves as in control of their own futures whereas those who do not attend church are more likely to see themselves as victims of oppression.[6]

The desperation for closeness with a missing father has driven some men to homosexuality, the subject of my first book. Data gathered over many decades has confirmed that children who live without their fathers are far more likely to do poorly in school and to be involved with drugs and other criminal behavior.

Why is this? Some bad behavior is tied, of course, to the anger and resentment that children feel who are abandoned by their dads. The rest, I believe, is tied to the role a father is supposed to fulfill. Every child needs a mother's touch, her nurturing hand, and warm embrace. Yet children need equally the boundaries and discipline which real men more naturally provide. The more fathers that are missing, the more children not only lack dads, but also grandfathers, uncles, and neighbors who show them how real men are supposed to behave.

It goes without saying that mothers play a crucial role in the development of children as well. However, the essential nature of the father's presence in his children's lives should put mothers on warning. Although a healthy marriage is the foundation of a healthy family, wives must never *compete* with their children or stepchildren for the father's attention and time. They must make sure the children get what they need, and address their own needs and wants with their husband at the appropriate time.

In addition to improving the outlook of children, the church has proven to support the overall strength of marriages as well. In fact, the more faithfully a couple attends church, the more likely they are to have a long-lasting stable marriage.[7] Regular attendance is even more important than a couple's specific denomination. Black Protestants have a divorce rate just as low as white Catholics.[8] All of this helps fathers remain in their children's lives where they belong.

In situations of divorce or when the mother and father were never married, mothers must keep the father out of the children's lives if there is legitimate concern regarding abuse, instability, or neglect. Otherwise she will serve her children best by helping them maintain a relationship with their father, not preventing or avoiding contact with him. This can be difficult when the mother has been hurt by the father, but she must not punish her children and thus curse the next generation because of her pain.

Now, I recognize that there are plenty of mothers who do their best to keep the father in the lives of their children, but it is the man who is either neglectful or inconsistent. In these cases we must trust the Lord to provide the right men of God in the church or extended family to assist as role models for the children. Still a child's connection with his or her biological father is important enough to fight for whenever possible.

EVERY LEVEL COUNTS

If we are to reverse the curse of fatherlessness in our generation we must begin to prioritize every level of fathering in our lives and the lives of our children. This means our relationship with our heavenly Father, our spiritual father, and our earthly or biological father who play a crucial role in our lives, in our ministries, and in our inheritance. A single mother can make sure that she is first in right relationship (to the best of her ability) with these three fathers in her life, and thus begin to lay the foundation for a better future for her kids.

We will never be able to have a healthy relationship with anyone else on this Earth if we are not connected to our heavenly Father through repentance and faith in the finished work of Jesus Christ. Our relationship with Him does not *replace* our relationship with our earthly and spiritual fathers, but it lays the foundation for all our relationships. A broken window or a hole in the wall can be repaired if the foundation of the building is secure, but a broken foundation will always lead to the collapse of the house.

There is only one real way to measure the success of the father—the character of his children. Now just because someone is visibly serving the Lord is no guarantee they will be a successful father. The Bible tells us that Eli was a great prophet, but a terrible father, "Now the sons of Eli were corrupt; they did not know the Lord" (1 Sam. 2:12). Samuel anointed the kings, "But his sons did not walk in his ways; they turned aside after dishonest gain, took bribes, and perverted justice" (1 Sam. 8:3). David was a man after God's own heart, but his son Absalom tried to seize power from him, dying tragically in battle (2 Sam. 18).

The church today is full of Elis and Samuels, speaking the Word of the Lord in front of the multitudes while their own children run wild in sin and rebellion. Successful ministry means nothing if we cannot raise our own children up to love and serve God. I keep that in mind everyday as I pastor my church, host my radio show, and travel around the country and the world to minister. None of my achievements mean anything if I neglect my own children.

There is another level of fathering that Scripture describes which we commonly call "spiritual fatherhood." This is the man who leads you to the Lord or plays a vital role in your spiritual growth and development. This person could be your natural father as well, but often it is a different individual. Paul was not married and had no biological children, but the Bible speaks of him begetting people in the Gospel: "For though you might have ten thousand instructors in Christ, yet you do not have many fathers; for in Christ Jesus I have begotten you through the gospel" (1 Cor. 4:15).

In 2 Timothy 1:2, Paul speaks of Timothy as a "dear son." In Titus 1:4, he speaks of Titus as a "true son." We need to understand today that Paul was not just throwing the term *son* around. He had many other associates that he never referred to that way. His letters tell us today about what it means to be a spiritual father to those God has entrusted to you.

Are You There, Dad?

In my experience as a pastor there were three general types of fathers for people growing up in my generation. For the purposes of discussion, I call them the Great Dads, the Workaholics, and the Absentees.

The Great Dads managed to take care of the family and be involved in our day-to-day growing up. They brought home the paycheck, kept a roof over our heads and food on the table. They also made it to most of those basketball games, took us fishing and taught us how to fix the car. In my experience, the people who grew up with these kinds of dads are more confident, proactive, and ready to face the challenges of life. They understand how to be patient and involved with their own children, because they are giving what they already received.

Then we have the Workaholics. These were the dads that got the job done: we were fed, taken care of, and sometimes even a little spoiled. Maybe Dad had to work two or even three jobs, but we had the shoes we needed. Yet his involvement was often just to give a distant approval or disapproval to our actions. If we got good grades or caught the game-winning touchdown, he might look up from his paper and give us a nod at the dinner table. If we got in trouble at school, you'd better believe the trouble we would face at home would be a lot scarier.

This was not a "fun" system with father-son hunting trips or a lot of hugs, but it did work. For the most part, people I meet raised by this kind of dad are driven for success. They might be haunted by a secret fear that they are not "good enough," but for the most part they do what they need to do. Unfortunately, many preachers fall into this category. They have somehow confused their ministries with their lives, and pour their best into the church while giving their wives and children leftovers. I wonder if the dads reading this book come home to spend more time playing with their kids and helping with their homework or watching TV, reading the sports section, or messing with the computer.

Unfortunately, the majority of black children in America have an Absentee as a dad. He might show up once a year to your birthday party, or drop you a call during the holidays. Maybe he was at your high school graduation or some other "important" day. When you were little, these little visits meant everything to you. You would think about his face for weeks before and after. But as you grew up, a pain in your heart—the pain of his rejection, his lack of involvement, his absence—became slowly unbearable.

I realize these little portraits are generalizations. Thousands of fathers at least exist somewhere between these examples. Still I think they offer a useful model to evaluate our own dads as well as ourselves. They can also help us understand how we feel and decide what to do about it.

Hope and Healing

I want to say right now that the cycle of fatherlessness can be broken. If you are a father who had an absentee dad, or even an abusive dad, you do not have to repeat that behavior with your own child. You need to know, however, that it will not be easy. You will have to fight to teach yourself what your father never taught you. It will feel unfair. It will feel too hard. It is not something you will resolve in a week, a month, or a year. This is a marathon, not a sprint.

In the next chapter, I will discuss the foundation for a spiritual and natural plan to break the curse of fatherlessness in your lineage. It is not something you do once or twice. It is a roadmap for changing your thinking, your habits, and your lifestyle.

4

FINDING THE FATHER

Healing a Generation

The eyes of the future are looking back at us and they are praying for us to see beyond our own time.

—TERRY TEMPEST WILLIAMS[1]

W E HAVE LOOKED at the devastating effects of fatherlessness in the past. Healing the hopelessness and hurt it causes is not easy. Yet thanks to the mercy and grace of the heavenly Father, it is possible.

GOD'S INTENTION FOR GENERATIONAL RELATIONSHIPS

If you have ever attempted drastic home improvements or watched television shows devoted to that subject, you know that any major change requires planning. No one takes a sledgehammer to a wall or starts pulling out plumbing without first consulting an architect to plan what the new room or house will look like. The plan makes it clear what stays and what goes.

To heal a people who have never experienced family the way God intended it, we need to look at His original blueprints for generational relationships. When we understand God's purpose for the connection between parents and children, we understand why it is so devastating when that purpose is not fulfilled. Furthermore, we can get a clearer picture of what God wants to restore back to each one of us.

Most everyone knows that children pick up habits and tendencies from their parents, but few understand the full impact of the generational blessings and curses that fathers pass to their sons and daughters. To fully comprehend the effect of a father's decisions on his children, we must first understand that God's plan for every lineage is generational increase:

> Then the Lord your God will bring you to the land, which your fathers possessed, and you shall possess it. He will prosper you and multiply you more than your fathers.
>
> —Deuteronomy 30:5

God wants each subsequent generation to build on what the previous generation has achieved. He wants children to be better educated and more prosperous than their parents, and to teach and train their own children to be more prosperous than themselves. This prosperity is not just financial by any means; it is spiritual, emotional, mental, and physical as well. When a father is leading his household effectively, these things will increase naturally, although not without effort.

Decades ago, fathers who never even made it to high school

worked hard in a factory or on a farm. They rented a little house but used what they saved to buy land and left it to their children. The next generation completed high school, became the manager at the plant or the factory and built houses on that land. They raised their children to study hard and make the most of their opportunities.

The next generation completed college. Some went on to graduate school and became doctors and lawyers. Others went into business or education. They were able to have a down-payment for a home two years after graduation. They could send their children to private school. They could travel the world.

This may sound too simple or even unrealistic, but it is the story of large numbers of black families after slavery. But what happens when a father abandons his role?

> When all that generation had been gathered to their fathers, another generation arose after them who did not know the Lord nor the work, which He had done for Israel. Then the children of Israel did evil in the sight of the LORD, and served the Baals; and they forsook the LORD God of their fathers, who had brought them out of the land of Egypt; and they followed other gods from among the gods of the people who were all around them, and they bowed down to them; and they provoked the LORD to anger. They forsook the LORD and served Baal and the Ashtoreths. And the anger of the LORD was hot against Israel. So He delivered them into the hands of plunderers who despoiled them; and

He sold them into the hands of their enemies all around, so that they could no longer stand before their enemies. Wherever they went out, the hand of the LORD was against them for calamity, as the LORD had said, and as the LORD had sworn to them. And they were greatly distressed.

—Judges 2:10–15

When the father forsakes his role as a channel of blessing for his children, the subsequent generation will often be worse off than their parents. A father and mother work hard in a factory or on a farm, but Dad has a drinking problem. He still brings home the paycheck, but he spends half his money on liquor and half his nights getting liquored up. Junior sees this. It makes him angry and embarrassed, but there's nothing he can do. Dad isn't keeping very close track of where Junior is as a teenager, and when he's seventeen he gets his girlfriend pregnant. They get married and manage to finish high school, but college is not happening. They both work, try to get their own apartment, and struggle to learn how to live as adults when they barely finished being kids.

After seven years, Junior has had it with marriage. They divorce and he moves across town near a better job. He sends money and comes by every week, which turns into every month, and after he meets a new girlfriend with a kid of her own, a couple times a year. He keeps his job, keeps it low key with his girlfriend, and thinks about his son. Junior's son is now fifteen. He misses his dad so much it aches. Only he's tired of the ache, so he puts on an attitude at school and at home so no one will know how hurt he feels.

Junior has no idea his son's friends are smoking weed, and that it's several times more potent than the weed he tried in high school. He has no idea that some older boys have been scoping out his son for their "import/export" business on the corner. He also has no idea his nephew has invited his son to a youth retreat next weekend. His son's destiny hangs in the balance, and Junior has no idea what's going on.

THE BLESSINGS OF THE SPIRITUAL FATHER

One of the ways that God has ordained to heal a generation of fatherless men and women is by connecting every one of His children with a spiritual father. A spiritual father cannot go back in time and make up for all those missed baseball games and birthday parties. God has to supernaturally heal that pain. However, a spiritual father can provide the counsel, correction, and guidance you need to become the man or woman God created you to be.

I know beyond a shadow of a doubt that I am successful in my life, my ministry, and my family because I have the blessing of my spiritual father. I take this so seriously that I believe that under no circumstances should a son or daughter leave his or her spiritual father. This charge to faithfulness is not for the sake of the father; it is for the sake of the son. Listen to the fifth commandment: "Honor your father and your mother, that your days may be long upon the land which the Lord your God is giving you" (Exod. 20:12). The benefit to honoring your spiritual father goes to you, not him.

The relationship between Elijah and Elisha offers the

clearest picture of the blessings available when we honor our spiritual fathers faithfully.

> And so it was, when they had crossed over, that Elijah said to Elisha, "Ask! What may I do for you, before I am taken away from you?" Elisha said, "Please let a double portion of your spirit be upon me." So he said, You have asked a hard thing. Nevertheless, if you see me when I am taken from you, it shall be so for you; but if not, it shall not be so." Then it happened, as they continued on and talked, that suddenly a chariot of fire appeared with horses of fire, and separated the two of them; and Elijah went up by a whirlwind into heaven. And Elisha saw it, and he cried out, "My father, my father, the chariot of Israel and its horsemen!" So he saw him no more. And he took hold of his own clothes and tore them into two pieces. He also took up the mantle of Elijah that had fallen from him, and went back and stood by the bank of the Jordan. Then he took the mantle of Elijah that had fallen from him, and struck the water, and said, "Where is the Lord God of Elijah?" And when he also had struck the water, it was divided this way and that; and Elisha crossed over.
>
> —2 Kings 2:9–14

We know from the Scriptures that Elisha went on to perform twice as many miracles as his spiritual father, Elijah. Yet despite these blessings, all kinds of people leave churches and spiritual fathers. They become bitter over the imperfections of others, while expecting those same people to overlook their own faults. In many cases, they may abandon the faith altogether. This is ironic, because often they have been hurt by other people violating biblical teaching. Why leave the God of the Bible who teaches that what those people did was wrong? The ethic of the world is "dog-eat-dog" and "fend for yourself." How is the world going to treat you better than people who are at least trying to follow the Bible?

A quick glance through the Word of God reveals numerous warnings about the curses that befall us if we leave our God-ordained spiritual fathers. Think about the story of the blessings showered on Elisha who remained faithful to Elijah, and compare it to the curses that befell Ham in Genesis 9 after he exposed Noah's drunkenness. Remember how Joshua and Caleb stuck with Moses through all the trials of the desert wandering and contrast it with the fate of Korah, Dathan, and Abiram who rebelled and complained. The Bible tells us:

> That the ground split apart under them, and the earth opened its mouth and swallowed them up, with their households and all the men with Korah, with all their goods. So they and all those with them went down alive into the pit; the earth closed over them, and they perished from among the assembly.
>
> —Numbers 16:31–33

These men and their families were swallowed up by the earth as an example of what can happen when you leave your spiritual father. Look at the life and legacy of Timothy, Paul's "dear son," versus the testimony of Demas who Paul said, "has forsaken me, having loved this present world" (2 Tim. 4:10).

It is important to remember that even the "Great Dads" we talked about in the last chapter are human and have disappointed their children. I am very aware that my weaknesses affect my natural children and my spiritual children, just as my own fathers' weaknesses affected me. Still, even in this, Jesus identified with mankind. He was rejected by His father, crying out on the cross, "My God, my God, why have You forsaken Me" (Matt. 27:46). Contrast His response with that of Satan, who simply felt like he wasn't getting enough recognition and decided to rebel.

We can be healed from the hurts of fatherlessness as we focus on the spirit of sonship (by which I mean daughtership as well). What is this spirit? The common factor among all the faithful sons in Scripture—Joshua, Caleb, Elisha, Timothy, and so on—is that they *served* their spiritual fathers. They did what their fathers needed them to do. They didn't get tangled up in the affairs of the world, and they did not waste time with their own vain pursuits.

Jesus said He only did what He saw His Father do. Elisha *saw* Elijah get taken up. If you can see eye to eye with the vision of your spiritual father, you too will know that blessing. Remember, serving and honoring your spiritual father blesses *you*. If you are not serving your spiritual father, you are only perpetuating more hurt in your own life.

FIVE PROVEN PRINCIPLES

I want to now lay the foundation for the "solutions" portion of this book by outlining five proven principles that will strengthen a father's ability to overcome the curse of fatherlessness.

1. There must be repentance: a change of mind.

The first step to becoming a better father is to repent for your sins. You must stop making excuses for yourself and ask God to change your heart and mind. Listen to this wonderful promise, "Repent therefore and be converted, that your sins may be blotted out, so that times of refreshing may come from the presence of the Lord" (Acts 3:19). The times of refreshing only come when we turn away from our sins and toward the Lord.

2. There must be a return: a change of direction.

Remember the story of the prodigal son? He changed his mind that moment in the pig sty when he realized how foolish he was. However, his change was not complete until he returned home. If you have strayed in your lifestyle as a father, you must return to the way you know is right. You must change the direction of your life.

3. There must be reconciliation: a change of relationships.

> Now all things are of God, who has reconciled us to Himself through Jesus Christ, and has given us the ministry of reconciliation, that is, that God was in Christ reconciling the world to Himself,

> not imputing their trespasses to them, and has
> committed to us the word of reconciliation.
>> —2 Corinthians 5:18–19

The next step as a father is to begin reconciling yourself to the people in your life that are most important. You can begin with your children, if there is any rupture in the relationship. If your parents are still living, you must attempt to reconcile with them if necessary. Although this can be very painful, it is a vital step to breaking the curse of fatherlessness.

4. There must be a restoring: a change of conditions.

Curses take a toll. Restoration means more than just getting sin and bad behavior right. It means changing the conditions around you to make the situation right. It means making you and those you have hurt whole again. Who can perform such a miracle except God? "So I will restore to you the years that the swarming locust has eaten" (Joel 2:25). God promises to restore to us what was lost when we meet His conditions, but we must take the steps to receive His restoration.

5. There must be a redeeming of time: a change of priorities.

If we are to raise up the Elishas of tomorrow, we must change our priorities. If we are to be worthy of the honor God commands our children to give us, we must make them a priority. "See then that you walk circumspectly, not as fools but as wise, redeeming the time, because the days are evil" (Eph. 5:15–16).

God desires that we know more than our fathers did by

learning from their mistakes while building on their successes. This cannot happen if we do not repent of our sins, return to the right way, and reconcile ourselves to the important people in our lives. You are then free to receive God's restoration and redeem the time to His glory.

5

WHY WE STILL NEED THE CHURCH

Challenges and Hope in Today's Black Church

*If a branch is broken from...a tree, it cannot bud; if a
stream is cut off from its source, it dries up...
Nor can he who forsakes the church of Christ attain to the
rewards of Christ. He is a stranger, he is an enemy.
Without the church for your mother, you cannot
have God for your Father.*

—CYPRIAN, THIRD-CENTURY THEOLOGIAN[1]

T HE BLACK CHURCH is a miracle. Why would slaves who
survived the Middle Passage and evils of plantation
slavery embrace the faith of their captors? Even more,
they understood the God of Abraham, Isaac, and Jacob to
be a Deliverer, crying out to Him for their freedom. After
Emancipation, as newly freed slaves moved to northern cities,
storefront churches sprang up on every corner, no matter how
dilapidated. They may have been heated by only a potbelly
stove, but they were warmed by the Holy Spirit.

During the Jim Crow era, the black church thrived as a
"house of hope," giving birth to the Civil Rights Movement

and its leaders. As African-Americans forged new opportunities for themselves in spite of the hostility they faced, they found affirmation and encouragement in their houses of worship. The black church has not only survived, but has been the bedrock of the black community for generations.

STILL THE HOPE OF THE WORLD

Now, in an era of greater opportunity than ever before, many black men have decided they don't need or want the church anymore. Postmodern thought has seduced some into believing that truth is relative and the Bible is unimportant. Yet I ask again: are the men who have left better off for their absence? Are they more prosperous? Are their marriages better? Are their children thriving?

I believe the church still holds the answer, because the answer is Jesus Christ. Jesus' teachings and salvation still offer the greatest source of hope, faith, and destiny for blacks and America as a whole. The Bible teaches that God has anointed black men to lead their families and, in their local churches, to bring that message of hope and faith to their communities. When they do not, the entire community suffers. Of course some may contend, like John Fountain does in his article, that we can be connected to God and Jesus' teachings without being connected to His church. The Bible tells a different story:

> And let us consider one another in order to stir up love and good works, not forsaking the assembling of ourselves together, as is the manner of some, but

> exhorting one another, and so much the more as
> you see the Day approaching.
>
> —Hebrews 10:24–25

The Bible also makes it clear that we cannot function as Christians apart from the rest of the body of Christ, which is the church. Romans 12:4–5 reminds us, "For as we have many members in one body, but all the members do not have the same function, so we, being many, are one body in Christ, and individually members of one another."

We cannot pay God lip service and forsake His church. For over twenty years, lack of church attendance in black men has been associated with increased criminal activity, drug use, and alcoholism.[2] Even non-religious people can see the value in religion in promoting social stability. Studies demonstrate that church attendance has a positive effect on the following areas:

- family strength;
- marital stability and happiness;
- poverty (young people classified as "poor" are far more likely to move out of poverty if they attend church regularly);
- personal moral standards and judgment;
- recovery from personal trauma.

In addition, those who attend church regularly are far less likely to commit suicide, abuse drugs, have a child out of wedlock, commit crimes, divorce, or become depressed.

In 1991, Allen Bergin, professor of psychology at Brigham Young University, summarized the effect of regular religious practice: "Such problems as sexual permissiveness, teen pregnancy, suicide, drug abuse, alcoholism, and to some extent deviant and delinquent acts [are reduced], and increases self-esteem, family cohesiveness, and general well-being."[3]

LOSING OURSELVES

We live in an increasingly diverse society where culture and race no longer mean what they did fifty years ago. I have served proudly alongside many white pastors in my community, and I appreciate the work that they do. I am glad that many of them are working to build multiethnic ministries, and that we are free to worship together across racial lines in a way that would have been impossible just a few generations ago.

However, I do want to observe that this new set of social circumstances presents the black church with a unique challenge. A few generations ago, circumstances and prejudice drove us together; no one else would "have" us. Now that we can feel free to go almost anywhere, some blacks choose to attend white-led churches. There is nothing wrong with this, but we must acknowledge the absence they leave in the black churches, particularly when they are educated and successful.

As the black church seeks to tackle the challenges in the black community, it needs as many positive examples and role models as it can get. When too many of those role models worship somewhere else, it can leave a gap in leadership.

There is a reoccurring and underlying trend among many blacks and their overly loyalty to churches led by white pastors.

Part of this trend is largely due to the fact that many blacks think that when they're doing better in life—promotion on the job, living in a better neighborhood, better schools for their children—that they should perhaps live and maybe even worship with the better and upper parts of society. Unfortunately, this isn't really anything new to African-Americans.

Many blacks may choose a church that has more expansive ministries for the entire family—children's church, couples' fellowships, civic, recreational, and social ministries. Today we can rejoice that many African-American churches have developed more comprehensive ministries that are sensitive to the ever-changing needs and priority of families. However, some still lag behind. Yet families should ask themselves not just what the church they are considering could do for them, but what they can contribute in service as well. Perhaps you are the one to improve the children's ministry, start a couple's fellowship, or organize a community outreach.

In a way, the black church is preserving the culture that preserved us all those generations. It is the guardian of the heritage of which we can be proud: our families and our perseverance as well as our music, food, and dance. Isn't this what we want America to see as the image of our community, in place of the destructive, misogynistic secular culture that has received so much media attention?

DOMINEERING WOMEN

The absence of the black man in home has given rise to another phenomenon: the domineering black woman. Now I do not mean to blame those who have been abandoned by their husbands or fathers for needing to take charge of their lives and their futures. However, if we are to reverse the trends of fatherlessness that we've discussed in earlier chapters, we must return to a biblical understanding of gender roles in the home and even in the church.

The bottom line is this: a church with aggressive unsubmitted women will not attract men. Period. Some high profile female preachers and evangelists have utilized an aggressive tone in their preaching and have become very successful ministering to women. However, I can't recall too many of these women that have built churches that attract large numbers of men. The fact that some of these ministers have been divorced once or even twice demonstrates that their philosophy may not build strong marriages either.

I realize that many black women are in a nearly impossible situation. Singles have to aggressively pursue their education and employment goals to survive without a husband. Single mothers often have to become both mom and dad to their children. I am not finding fault with any godly responses to those circumstances. However, the church must be the place where believers in all situations can see a model of how marital and family life should be. Children from single parent homes should come and seen functional families worshiping together. Singles should see wives submitting to their husbands and children submitting to their parents according to the Word of God:

> Wives, submit to your own husbands, as to the Lord. For the husband is head of the wife, as also Christ is head of the church; and He is the Savior of the body.

> Therefore, just as the church is subject to Christ, so
> let the wives be to their own husbands in everything.
> Husbands, love your wives, just as Christ also loved
> the church and gave Himself for her.
>
> —Ephesians 5:22–25

I know that many black women would love for their husbands (or the boyfriends they hope will become their husbands) to take a more active leadership role in planning the family's future. However, many such women would do well to realize that the way to get a man to do his job is not by nagging him or arguing with him to do it. That will often encourage him to become even more passive and apathetic, or to strike back in a combative manner.

Although some black women have succumbed to the notion of "male-hating," declaring proudly that they don't need a man for anything, I believe most are simply frustrated. The media is in love with the stereotypical loud and brassy black woman, playing it for laughs. However, the directors and screenwriters aren't there to counsel the young women who see those fictional characters as models of success. They think they can strut their stuff, sleep around, be a professional success, and have a full life. Yet many others ache in their hearts for a husband and children. Will humorous, aggressive mannerisms teach these women how to be good wives and mothers?

The scriptural requirements for wives may not be very popular but they are still right:

Wives, likewise, be submissive to your own husbands, that even if some do not obey the word, they, without a word, may be won by the conduct of their wives, when they observe your chaste conduct accompanied by fear. Do not let your adornment be merely outward—arranging the hair, wearing gold, or putting on fine apparel—rather let it be the hidden person of the heart, with the incorruptible beauty of a gentle and quiet spirit, which is very precious in the sight of God. For in this manner, in former times, the holy women who trusted in God also adorned themselves, being submissive to their own husbands, as Sarah obeyed Abraham, calling him lord, whose daughters you are if you do good and are not afraid with any terror. Husbands, likewise, dwell with them with understanding, giving honor to the wife, as to the weaker vessel, and as being heirs together of the grace of life, that your prayers may not be hindered.

—1 Peter 3:1–7

Christian wives demonstrate the reality of God by the way they treat their husbands. We need churches full of women who model this kind of submission and teach young girls what it means to be a godly wife. When men who are outside the church see wives in the church respecting their husbands, it will make the house of God a much more welcoming place for them.

Restoring Manhood to Black Men

Leanne Payne observed in her book, *Crisis in Masculinity*, "We cannot pass on to the next generation what we do not ourselves possess. Unaffirmed men are unable adequately to affirm their own sons and daughters as male and female and therefore as persons."[4]

There are few things in this world that make me feel as ashamed as the pompous and flamboyant behavior of effeminate black men. I find it a thousand times more embarrassing in the church. There was a time when feminine speech, jewelry, dress, and mannerisms were nearly unheard of among black men. Now, generations of boys raised without fathers are wandering around acting like women.

Boys must have their masculinity affirmed by their fathers. Our Lord Jesus Christ was affirmed by the Father in heaven when He was baptized in the Jordan River. God said, "This is my beloved Son in whom I am well pleased" (Matt. 3:17). When the biological father is missing, boys must be affirmed by a male relative or role model in the church.

There are many people who would have us believe that there is nothing wrong with these boys who suffer from gender confusion. Payne continues, "An automatic and serious consequence of a man's failure to be affirmed in his masculinity is that he will suffer from low self-esteem. He will be unable to accept himself...The masculine qualities and gifts are there, but they have not been 'affirmed' into life."[5]

Pastors who allow effeminate men to sing in the choir or otherwise minister in their churches may feel like they are being open-minded. Maybe they just want to utilize the best talent. Whatever their reasons, they are using men for ministry who are in need of ministry themselves. God has a plan for healing and wholeness for the man who struggles with his masculinity or even with homosexual feelings.

Furthermore, the presence of effeminate men in a church (who are not receiving ministry to bring them to healing) will repel masculine men who might otherwise be inclined to attend. The wife or girlfriend of a man who *is* affirmed in his masculinity to some degree will not have much success persuading him to come to a church full of "sissies." The black church can no longer afford to ignore this issue. We must recognize these "gender issues" for what they are: a terrible consequence of absent fathers that needs to be confronted by the church and healed by God.

Payne continues, "Psychologists have long pointed out that the progression from infancy to maturity involves many steps of psychosocial development, and when we miss one of these we are in trouble. The step of self-acceptance ideally comes just after puberty. The key to taking this step, on the ordinary human level, lies in the love and affirmation of a whole father. Just as the mother is so vital in those first months of life, so is the father in this later period. No matter how whole the mother is psychologically and spiritually, she cannot bridge the gap left by the missing father."[6]

As I've stated previously in my book *Straight Up: The Church's Official Response to the Epidemic of Down-Low Living,* fatherlessness has led to an epidemic in homosexual behavior, even among men who consider themselves hetero-sexual. From pop culture to TV shows, movies, media coverage, and government policy, the down-low terminology and lifestyle have crept secretly into the mainstream black American landscape.

R. Kelly's *Trapped in the Closet* portrays a male pastor deceptively involved with another man in a homosexual relationship. The recently released movie, *On the Down Low*, introduces us to Angel and Isaac, two male gangbangers on the south side of Chicago that have developed a homosexual relationship although they are members of rivaling gangs. Then, there's *Invisible*, a movie whose main character is a married father who eventually sleeps with his male neighbor, another homosexual man.

Recently, J. Lee Grady, editor of *Charisma* magazine expressed his disapproval of *Brokeback Mountain*, an Oscar-winning movie about two closeted homosexual cowboys from the northwest who eventually fight through the pressures of families to be reunited with each other. Like Grady, I can't decide which was worse: the movie itself celebrating homosexuality or the fact that America received it as one of the year's most beautiful films.

As is so often the case, life has begun to imitate art. Author Terry McMillan has filed for divorce from the man who inspired the 1996 novel *How Stella Got Her Groove Back*, which detailed the romantic adventures of a forty-something woman who falls for a guy half her age. In papers filed in Contra Costa County Superior Court, McMillan, age fifty-three, says she decided to end her six-year marriage to Jonathan Plummer, age thirty, after learning he is a homosexual.

McMillan met Plummer at a Jamaican resort a decade ago. "It was devastating to discover that a relationship I had publicized to the world as life-affirming and built on mutual love was actually based on deceit," she said in court papers. "I was humiliated." In response, Plummer maintained McMillan treated him with "homophobic" scorn bordering on harassment since he came out to her as gay just before Christmas.

From *Oprah* to *Ebony*, African-American men on the down-low have become the new traveling freak show for the entire nation to gape at. Former Clinton White House aide Keith Boykens gave down-low living a more scholarly treatment in *Beyond the Down Low*. Although a thoughtful work that gives a historical account of homosexuality and bisexuality within the African-American race, in the end it is just another tired rationalization of his homosexual lifestyle. My question is, "Is there any balm of healing for Boykens, Plummer, McMillan, R. Kelly, and any person that is living a desperate life of shame, brokenness, and pain?"[7]

TURNING THE TIDE

No More Excuses

Every system is perfectly designed to get the results it gets.

—SOURCE UNKNOWN

S O WHY AREN'T more black men in church? For that matter, why do so many get an attitude when you invite them to go? In one sense, maybe we shouldn't be too surprised that the black men who are rebelling against God don't want to gather each week to worship Him. But if these are the people the African-American church is called to reach, we have to ask ourselves why we are not doing a better job.

David Murrow's book *Why Men Hate Going to Church* suggests, "Today's church has developed a culture that is driving men away Almost every man in America has tried church, but two-thirds find it unworthy of a couple of hours once a week."[1] Clearly many black men find little with which to connect in the average neighborhood church. Whether it's the music, the frowning ushers, or the lack of excitement, many would rather sleep in and watch football. It wasn't always this way.

There was a time when the church was the undisputed cornerstone of the black community. Black businesses were born out of church congregations, and civil rights protests were organized in sanctuaries. Yet over the past two generations, there is a growing perception that the church is no longer addressing the needs of the people outside its walls. The influence of the pulpit is no longer reaching into the neighborhood. The preacher's words lose their relevance at the sanctuary doors.

During much of the twentieth century, the Nation of Islam (along with other pseudo-Islamic black groups) has capitalized on the church's lessening influence. They have actively recruited young men in prisons. They have preached a message of self-reliance and self-respect that appears to fill a need in these men's lives. It is not a feminine message. In decades past they were known to mobilize those men, in some cities at least, to provide a sense of order in the midst of chaos. While official numbers are hard to come by, anecdotal evidence suggests they have had no trouble attracting young masculine men into their organization.

As Christians, it is easy to gather to preach and pray about the social issues facing our community. It is much harder to roll up our sleeves and become involved. I believe we have to do both. The church should be at the forefront of the battle for the safety of our cities and the success of our schools, and I will discuss many of the practical steps we can take to restore our relevance to the needs of the hour. At the same time, we cannot forget that many of these social problems will not be solved with social action alone. It will take the supernatural intervention of God to heal hearts and change lives.

FEMINIZING THE GOSPEL

Asking how women came to dominate so much of the life of the modern black church can be a bit like asking which came first, the chicken or the egg. Did women dominate first and then the men left, or did men leave and then women came to dominate? It was most likely a little of both. However we got here, the result is that many men do not feel comfortable or welcome, and our pews are filled with women.

It is impossible to discuss the absence of black men from church without addressing the need to make church feel masculine. Think about a young black boy's perception of church. Most likely, his mother is the one who takes him, not his father. Most likely he sees a choir filled with women, female ushers, and his Sunday school or children's church teacher is likely female as well. Add to that the fact that it is likely his mother who prays with him at night (if anyone does) and tells him to read his Bible, and he has concluded by the time he is old enough to stay at home by himself that church is for women and kids. Paul talked about putting childish things away when he became a man (1 Cor. 13:11). Well, for today's black man, those "childish things" just might include church.

Think about the "Sunday school Jesus" many of us recognized as the only Jesus of the Bible. We saw the image in Sunday school and Vacation Bible School materials over the years. These pictures were the same ones decorating the foyers and fellowship halls of many churches—a very calm and gentle looking man with long hair and rosy cheeks.

As Murrow challenges us, is this the Jesus we want our young boys to remember and model themselves after? What about when a young man is ready to leave adolescence and wants to put those childish things behind him? What will he abandon first? Murrow suggests that 70 percent of young men of all races who grew up in the church will leave the church by the age of twenty and many will never return.[2]

Now what about the grown black man who might give church another try, probably to appease his wife or girlfriend? Does he see a potential spiritual father in the pulpit, or does he see an unapproachable man insulated by expensive suits, a Rolex watch, and a Rolls Royce in the parking lot? Maybe he hears music that stirs a sense of excitement and anticipation, but more than likely he hears a hymn that reminds him of his grandmother. Come to think of it, so do all the flowers and the pastel colors in the sanctuary!

What about the announcements? If he chooses to listen, will he hear about any activity that interests him? Chances are, he's not too thrilled about the fundraiser for the new carpets or a prayer meeting where a bunch of women cry and scream. Add an aggressive offering message that sounds like it's pressuring him to give up that twenty dollar bill in his pocket, and he's completely tuned out before the pastor even gets up to preach.

These are a few of the many reasons that a grown man might never come to church voluntarily during his adult life. As I've already shared, it doesn't mean the church has nothing to offer him. It just means the package they have it in does not inspire him to check it out.

Now there is one more scenario that is all too common these days. In most cases it will cause that man to vow never to return to church again. What if after he's listened to the sermon, passed the collection plate, and returned to his regular life, he hears about that pastor again? But this time he hears that pastor is sleeping with his secretary, or he reads in the paper that he's been embezzling money from the church. More often than not, he will use that man's fall as an excuse to stay away forever.

In his 1994 book *Adam, Where Are You?: Why Most Black Men Don't Go to Church*, Dr. Jawanza Kunjufu, noted these and several other reasons black men don't seem to go to church anymore. He mentions that many of the fatherless men we discussed transfer their anger with their biological fathers to anger with God. Having never been taught to submit to a father's loving leadership, they struggle to submit to spiritual authority.[3]

Whatever the reason black men don't want to come to church, that's exactly where God wants them to go. And that's exactly why we need to figure out how to get them there.

OPENING THE DOORS

And as He walked by the Sea of Galilee, He saw Simon and Andrew his brother casting a net into the sea; for they were fishermen. Then Jesus said to them, "Follow Me, and I will make you become fishers of men." They immediately left

their nets and followed Him. When He had gone
a little farther from there, He saw James the son
of Zebedee, and John his brother, who also were
in the boat mending their nets. And immediately
He called them, and they left their father Zebedee
in the boat with the hired servants, and went
after Him.

—Mark 1:16–20

What was it about Jesus that caused these men to drop
everything they were doing to follow Him? How can our
churches recapture that anointing as we reach out to today's
African-American man? Consider King David, who led thousands of men in extremely challenging circumstances:

And David numbered the people who were with
him, and set captains of thousands and captains
of hundreds over them. Then David sent out one
third of the people under the hand of Joab, one
third under the hand of Abishai the son of Zeruiah,
Joab's brother, and one third under the hand of
Ittai the Gittite. And the king said to the people,
"I also will surely go out with you myself." But the
people answered, "You shall not go out! For if we
flee away, they will not care about us; nor if half of
us die, will they care about us. But you are worth
ten thousand of us now. For you are now more
help to us in the city."

—2 Samuel 18:1–3

David's leadership did more than inspire men to come to a gathering. It motivated them to risk their lives for the cause of the kingdom. We know that the hundreds that gathered to follow him when he was still hiding out in a cave were not particularly impressive. They were desperate and debt-ridden, and some were on the run from the law (1 Sam. 22:1–2). Yet he was able to turn these distressed men into a mighty army. He understood how men thought and felt and offered a vision that would turn their lives around.

UNDERSTANDING ANGER

To reach today's black men, we must understand the centrality of overcoming the anger and disappointment that hold many of them captive. David's leadership of his army was validated by the fact that he had conquered anger and resentment in his own life:

> And when king David came to Bahurim, behold, thence came out a man of the family of the house of Saul, whose name was Shimei, the son of Gera: he came forth, and cursed still as he came. And he cast stones at David, and at all the servants of king David: and all the people and all the mighty men were on his right hand and on his left. And thus said Shimei when he cursed, Come out, come out, thou bloody man, and thou man of Belial: The LORD hath returned upon thee all the blood of the house of Saul, in whose stead thou hast reigned; and the LORD hath delivered the kingdom into the hand of

Absalom thy son: and, behold, thou art taken in thy mischief, because thou art a bloody man. Then said Abishai the son of Zeruiah unto the king, Why should this dead dog curse my lord the king? let me go over, I pray thee, and take off his head. And the king said, What have I to do with you, ye sons of Zeruiah? so let him curse, because the LORD hath said unto him, Curse David. Who shall then say, Wherefore hast thou done so? And David said to Abishai, and to all his servants, Behold, my son, which came forth of my bowels, seeketh my life: how much more now may this Benjamite do it? let him alone, and let him curse; for the LORD hath bidden him. It may be that the LORD will look on mine affliction, and that the LORD will requite me good for his cursing this day. And as David and his men went by the way, Shimei went along on the hill's side over against him, and cursed as he went, and threw stones at him, and cast dust. And the king, and all the people that were with him, came weary, and refreshed themselves there.

—2 Samuel 16:5–14, 19:16–23

Shimei was cursing David and throwing rocks at him in front of his entire army. Now David was the king of Israel at this time, so it was beyond outrageous for Shimei to brazenly insult and threaten him. In response, one of David's men offered to cut Shimei's head off to defend David's honor. After all, who would dare treat a king like that? Then David, the king of all Israel refused.

David was personally secure enough to know that he did not need to retaliate to prove anything. He understood that you will never defeat the one who curses you by cursing him back. This is what men today need to understand, and they need Davids who will show them the way. Like most people who have been in ministry for any length of time, I have been betrayed. I carry some scars from stab wounds inflicted when I least expected them.

Yet in it all God has taught me to bless my enemies. Instead of retaliating, He has taught me to buy them dinner. I have always spoken words of blessing and kindness over them, and there is no one to this day that I have to avoid or from whom I have to hide my face. I have not burned bridges, because I understand that my work is all about the kingdom.

Sometimes your blessings remind others what they could have had if they made other choices. If they take out their anger or frustration on you, you cannot take it personally. Saul tried to kill David and yet David was determined to show kindness to all the members of Saul's household forever (2 Sam. 16:1–4). Men today will only be set free by Christians who understand and practice forgiveness in their own lives.

The church has the answer to the anger and bitterness with which so many black men struggle. The black men who are in church demonstrate this fact. Sociologist Patrick Fagan points out, "It turns out that the practice of religion has a significant effect on happiness and an overall sense of personal well-being. Religious affiliation and regular church attendance are near the top of the list for most people in explaining their own happiness and serve as good predictors of who is most likely to have this sense of well-being. Happiness is greater and psychological stress is lower for those who attend religious services regularly."[4]

EXERCISING PATIENCE

We must understand that God is after men's hearts. He does not want men to just come to church to please their wives and girlfriends. He wants men who seek Him with authenticity. It will take time to win the hearts and minds of the men in your family and community to God's vision for their lives and the vision of your local church. It will take time to build their trust and confidence in your leadership and your pastor's leadership.

David had crowds of men following him in his cave because of his dynamic vision. "He won over the hearts of all the men of Judah as though they were one man!" (2 Sam. 19:14). Yet our patience will pay off. Once we begin to win men to the vision of God, that vision will become contagious. When we bring women into the church, we are often just adding to our numbers, but when we bring men we will multiply. This involves a greater investment over the short term, but offers a much greater harvest in the end.

Paul understood this and exhorted Timothy, "Thou therefore, my son, be strong in the grace that is in Christ Jesus. And the things that thou hast heard of me among many witnesses, the same commit thou to faithful men, who shall be able to teach others also" (2 Tim. 2:1–2).

When you have won the hearts of men, it is no longer necessary to try to order them around or manipulate them. When their hearts are submitted to the vision of God, a renewed passion for Him begins to motivate everything they do. If the church is to be the hope of the world—and particularly of urban black America—there will have to arise an army of men who can righteously take their places of authority and responsibility. Like David's army they may begin the journey distressed and in debt, but they will finish with victory.

WINNING THE HEARTS OF MEN

Creating a Culture in the Church That Reaches Black Men

The church has lost its place at the table of cultural relevancy.

—GEORGE BARNA[1]

ULTURE CAN BE defined in many ways. When we talk about the subculture of a particular organization, we usually mean the emotional and psychological environment. We mean the atmosphere that we sense when we enter a place and the unspoken communication of the people.

It has been said that cultures begin as fads that become trends, which form societies, cultures, and generations. Considering that our God sees all time at once, I like to think of our culture this way: what values do I want affirmed for my grandchildren? They are the ones who have to live in the world that I create for them. What can I do to make my family, church, community, and world a place that will welcome them, teach them how to live, and protect and treasure their lives? Terry Tempest Williams observed, "The eyes of the future are looking back at us and they are praying for us to see beyond our own time."[2]

Trailblazing minister and author David Murrow has been sounding the alarm for years about men of all races abandoning church. He points out that "Jesus had no trouble captivating men. Fishermen dropped nets full of fish to follow Him, but today's church can't convince men to drop their TV remote controls for a couple of hours a week."[3] I thank God for the passion and dedication of men like Murrow to call our brothers back the house of God. I agree with him that we have to be willing to part with some of our customs and habits to see them return.

I believe we must create a new culture within the black church. This culture must attract black men without compromising God's standards. This culture must provide a "safe haven" where these men can express themselves as they learn about God's plan for them and their families.

Jesus did not become like the world to save it, but He did speak in terms the world could understand. A short, balding, white football coach doesn't become "black" to communicate with the three hundred-pound offensive lineman on his team. However, he does speak to them about things that matter to them and inspires them to action. I want to outline some practical ways the church can begin to do that for African-American men.

BE MASCULINE

Most churches could open up a spa, a nail salon, or a shopping mall and do fantastic business. Typically, our churches are currently perfectly designed to give us exactly what we have—pews full of women. At the same time many offer little to stir the masculine heart, so consequently men find it dull and unappealing. Some have observed that the more masculine a man is, the more likely he is to dislike most churches. This is a completely counter-productive trend.

I am not saying that feminine things have no place in the church, nor am I discounting the need for women's ministry. After all, many hard-working, faithfully praying women are the reason we still have a church to talk about today. I am just saying that we need to balance feminine qualities with masculine ones if we want to change our results. If we want our churches to be at least half men, then each of our feminine activities and motifs should have a masculine counterpart.

BE APPROACHABLE

Pastors, along with all those who serve in their churches, should minimize the distance between themselves and the laymen in the church as well as the visitors. Congregations should be as welcoming to newcomers as possible. What man who has been out of church for ten or twenty years wants to come to a place where he is glared at for sitting in the wrong pew? I'll bet he doesn't want to be greeted by a frowning usher or a rude children's church volunteer either.

It is very easy for people who have belonged to a church for a while to become territorial about the ministry in which they serve. While many volunteers work hard and contribute invaluably to the church's operation, they must never forget for whom they are really working. We do not honor Jesus with our service if we insult or ignore the very people He is trying to reach through us!

Pastors and other leaders should consider Jesus' own example:

"You are my friends if you do what I command…I no longer call you servants…instead, I call you friends" (John 15:14–15). Of course, pastors need to carry themselves in a manner that is both holy and mature. Those that go beyond this to send off subtle signals that they cannot be bothered with "unimportant people" betray their insecurity. If the Son of God could be bothered with "the least of these," surely you can too!

Now this does not mean that the senior pastor has to do everything or hang out with everyone in the church. That is the responsibility of the entire leadership team. Relationships are the cornerstone of the twenty-first century church and no one can build a relationship with someone with whom they are afraid to strike up a conversation.

Approachability needs to be a leadership team effort that will reach more people and ultimately produce more leaders. The pastoral team cultivates an atmosphere in the entire congregation of openness and vulnerability. When people see that the leaders are humble and welcoming, they will learn to follow their example.

BE RELEVANT

To reach and disciple more men, we must seek opportunities to become more relevant in their lives. Consider Jesus: "Then He selected twelve of them to be his regular companions" (Mark 3:14, NLT). These were regular men, and yet Jesus invited them not just to follow Him, or to serve Him, but to share His life. They were pretty messed up when they started out and yet they belonged to Him. They were comfortable in His group.

We need to remember that all of us have areas where we are

growing. Do we allow others to feel comfortable in our midst before they have their beliefs and behavior in order? As many have asked, does someone belong before they believe? Jesus said yes. He welcomed sinners and disciples in various stages of growth long before they got their acts together. To address men where their needs are right now, we need to do the same.

BE EXCITING

I realize I am being somewhat controversial when I say that we should make our churches places of entertainment, excitement, and intrigue. After all, isn't entertainment worldly? Remember that entertainment doesn't just mean movies and television. It can simply mean to captivate or hold someone's attention. Isn't Jesus captivating? Entertainment can mean showing hospitality to someone in your home, a quality God commands of church leaders (1 Tim. 3:2).

Excitement can mean feeling cheerful joy (Acts 8:8). Shouldn't we experience that in church? Think about the feeling when you walk into a basketball arena before a big playoff game. Beyond the bright lights and loud music, the air is saturated with a sense of anticipation before the team even makes its appearance. What if our services could capture that kind of anticipation for what God is about to do?

Intrigue means to fascinate or to arouse someone's curiosity or interest. Church should awaken curiosity. People should not find more interesting discussions in the book store, university, or the coffee shop. Paul was so deep in his discussion of the Scriptures that many people could hardly understand what he was talking about. He could discuss truth with the most educated rabbis or the most charismatic philosophers of his day:

> And it came to pass, that he went through the corn fields on the sabbath day; and his disciples began, as they went, to pluck the ears of corn. And the Pharisees said unto him, Behold, why do they on the sabbath day that which is not lawful? And he said unto them, Have ye never read what David did, when he had need, and was an hungred, he, and they that were with him? How he went into the house of God in the days of Abiathar the high priest, and did eat the shewbread, which is not lawful to eat but for the priests, and gave also to them which were with him? And he said unto them, The sabbath was made for man, and not man for the sabbath: Therefore the Son of man is Lord also of the sabbath. And he entered again into the synagogue; and there was a man there which had a withered hand. And they watched him, whether he would heal him on the sabbath day; that they might accuse him. And he saith unto the man which had the withered hand, Stand forth. And he saith unto them, Is it lawful to do good on the sabbath days, or to do evil? to save life, or to kill? But they held their peace. And when he had looked round about on them with anger, being grieved for the hardness of their hearts, he saith unto the man, Stretch forth thine hand. And he stretched it out: and his hand was restored whole as the other.
>
> —Mark 2:23–3:6

Jesus reminded His disciples that the Sabbath was made for men, not the other way around. The church service is to honor God, but it is for the people that come. Almost everything about Jesus' life challenged the religious tradition of the day. It was not that the tradition itself was wrong, but the fact that it had come to overshadow the purpose for which the tradition was started in the first place.

No one wants to keep coming to a church service that is a glorified funeral. We need to be open to the Lord's ways of adding entertainment, excitement, and intrigue to our gatherings.

BE AUTHENTIC

Don't be a hypocrite! The essence of hypocrisy is not having a high standard, but rather demanding a high standard from others that you do not meet yourself. Christians that are real, transparent, and truthful will draw even the most hardened sinners. This doesn't mean there will never be times for correction and rebuke, but that should not be done publicly. We will not see men flooding our pews if we humiliate them, criticize them, or dishonor them in front of others.

Christians who can be honest about their past challenges and struggles will be able to guide and encourage those who are struggling now. People need to not only understand how great it is to live as a Christian but to learn about the journey that got them to where they are. You also must be willing to share your struggles, whether they are financial, or related to your marriage or family. Otherwise people feel like you are not subject to the pressures of this life. They will either not be able to relate to you, or they will be intimidated by you.

> I am the good shepherd. The good shepherd lays down his life for the sheep. The hired hand is not the shepherd who owns the sheep. So when he sees the wolf coming, he abandons the sheep and runs away. Then the wolf attacks the flock and scatters it. The man runs away because he is a hired hand and cares nothing for the sheep.
>
> —John 10:11–13

It has been said that men would rather see a sermon than hear a sermon. I agree. Let your unspoken lifestyle convict the men that begin to come into your church, rather than a constant barrage of criticism or faultfinding. Once we have patiently built a trusting relationship with them, we will be able to bring correction and rebuke when necessary.

BE MODEST

Many Christians could stand to have a greater sense of modesty with their financial blessings. There was time when modesty was considered part of Christian character; you were not supposed to show off what you had. At times it was taken to the extreme where pastors were supposed to be poor, and being spiritual meant being broke. This was completely counter-productive; pastors cannot lead effectively if they are in a constant state of need.

However, few would deny that the opposite extreme exists

today. Some high-profile ministers are living extravagant life-styles and flaunting their possessions as evidence of God's favor. This offends many men outside the church, even if their sports heroes and entertainment icons do the same thing.

Christians need to strike a balance by making wise financial choices and exercising restraint with their purchases. From the beginning of our ministry, my wife and I knew we didn't want to be the only ones in the church with a house of a particular size or a car of a particular make. There are some things we could have bought earlier in our lives but we waited until more people in our congregation were able to have them, too. If we have the attitude that we want everyone to be blessed, we will find God's blessing poured out in an even greater measure.

BE CONSIDERATE

I grew up with church services that lasted several hours and I understand that those kinds of traditions can be very hard to break. However, I have learned that if we are going to reach the unchurched, and men in particular, we must become more considerate of their time.

While I also recognize the value of wearing your "Sunday best" to show honor to God, we must make sure that our effort to honor God does not discourage others from getting to know Him. We should never stare disapprovingly at a visitor who seems to be dressed inappropriately. If you don't have time to build a relationship with someone to lovingly help him with his attire, you certainly don't have time to criticize.

Again, agreeing with and gleaning from some of Murrow's

practical suggestions from his book, *Why Men Hate Going to Church*, there are other practical ways to make our services more accommodating to those who are growing in their commitment:

- Shorten the worship time as well as the sermon to twenty minutes each. Remember that most men have an attention span of six to eight minutes; maximize the amount they absorb by keeping things moving.
- Preach on practical subjects that men can immediately apply to their everyday lives. Teach in a logical manner that everyone can follow, rather than being overly emotional.
- Remember to use illustrations that center on sports, adventure, the outdoors, and so on. These do not have to be your only illustrations, but don't forget to include them.
- Have a "men's huddle" with the men on Sunday after service for three minutes. Use this brief time for the men to connect with one another and discuss plans for the week.
- Use a little humor from time to time—men love humor.
- Have a few Sundays now and then when you encourage men to wear what they want. You could also have a "theme" Sunday: jerseys, old school/throwback clothes, clothes relating to occupations, and so on.

- Don't let Sunday be the only time your men see each other. Start or grow your small group ministry.
- Don't beat men up in the church for being bad fathers and husbands. As I've mentioned, there is a time for correction and rebuke, and the pulpit is generally the wrong time.
- Do not pressure men who are not members of the church to give offerings. Of course it is ridiculous that some men will drop two hundred dollars for game tickets and whine about giving twenty dollars at church, but give them time to grow.

BE COURAGEOUS

Be courageous and release your men for creative ministry! I have seen tremendous growth in my congregation as I have allowed the men to step out in their areas of gifting, passion, and expertise. I have been asked by colleagues what I would do if these men became so successful in their lay ministry that they started out on their own and split the church. I reply that I've already released them. As long as they start their ministry the right way, I will bless them to do so.

I love to commission the men in my church to do Monday through Saturday what I do on Sunday. My ministry is only successful if it is being reproduced in others. Remember the camaraderie and fellowship of the early church:

All the believers were together and had everything in common. Selling their possessions and goods, they gave to anyone as he had need. Every day they continued to meet together in the temple courts. They broke bread in their homes and ate together with glad and sincere hearts, praising God and enjoying the favor of all the people. And the Lord added to their number daily those who were being saved.

—Acts 2:44–47

We can regain that power and unity if we release our men to serve and lead ministries and small groups in areas of their strengths, interests and hobbies. Here are a few practical suggestions for ministries:

- sports ministry
- hunting/fishing small group ministry
- business start-up or consulting ministry
- free auto-mechanic weekend ministry
- weightlifting or workout ministry
- motorcycle-riding ministry

There is an element missing today from many churches throughout America, especially the larger, more progressive *mega* churches. This element is nothing new, but is essential to the development and deliverance of the men—the ministry of authentic supernatural healing. We must never assume that basketball, political advocacy, and men-huddles alone can heal and strengthen the men of the church. If the hearts and souls of men cannot be won over through continual committed prayer, then the practical programs, fun, and fellowship meetings are in vain. Not only should we be praying and interceding for these men, but we must emphasize in our teaching that they become men of prayer themselves. They should become men who not only pray, but are given to prayer. A dedicated and determined life of prayer is the ongoing process of man dying to his sins, habits, and frailties.

Coupled with teaching men to give themselves to prayer must be a vision consistently offering healing and deliverance opportunities. Whether it's a returning to "tarry days," or extended altar-call experiences, there must be time invested and an atmosphere cultivated to cast out demons, lay hands on the afflicted, and war in the spirit as necessary. Churches must take God's mandate seriously to prioritize the ministry of healing and deliverance from past and present sin, bitterness, bondages, and hurts.

Unfortunately, many of today's churches have abandoned deliverance in favor of going home early. Unlike the old days of tarrying services and extended times of altar ministry, many men today come to church and leave without any real confrontation. As I've mentioned, there is nothing wrong with being considerate of time in your Sunday morning services. However, we must also offer time at the altars for deliverance and change, whether it be a shut-in or all-night service, or an extended mid-week time.

Like many churches across the country, our church conducts quarterly Encounter Retreats for men who desire to attend. In fact, it is our church's expectation that all men who receive the Lord attend these spiritually intense retreats on a regular basis.

These events consist of three days and two nights at a remote conference center or lodge setting that is strategically designed for men to have a divine and lasting encounter with God.

Strategically, the men are removed from all family affairs and daily distractions. There are no televisions, computers, cell phones, or pagers. These retreats are designated times of intense spiritual warfare led by seasoned and experienced men of God who have consecrated themselves with fasting and prayer and prayed over the names of participants for several weeks before the actual event begins. Leaders provide ministry in several different settings, including small coaching groups, one-on-one mentoring, and group altar calls. Preaching and teaching centers on personal healing from past hurts, abuses and bondages, including sexual abuse, depression, witchcraft, rebellion, bitterness, and so on.

It is common during such events to see demons cast out, oppressive and generational spirits broken, and men completely set free. On Sunday morning, the retreat concludes by leading men back to the cross of Christ for forgiveness and receiving the baptism of the Holy Spirit. I can promise you that Sunday morning services will never be the same once you have welcomed back twenty or thirty men from such an experience!

I want to encourage every believer that God has not changed His mind about today's black men. God is waiting to bless them, and the vehicle He has chosen to use is the church. We must incline our ears to Him and follow His lead.

RENEWING THE COVENANT

A Commitment to Reach Our Communities

*If there is no struggle, there is no progress. Those who profess
to favor freedom and yet deprecate agitation, are men who
want crops without plowing up the ground, they want rain
without thunder and lightning. They want the ocean without
the awful roar of its many waters. This struggle may be a
moral one, or it may be a physical one, and it may be both
moral and physical, but it must be a struggle. Power concedes
nothing without a demand...It never did and it never will!*

—FREDERICK DOUGLAS[1]

LIKE MANY OTHERS, I read Tavis Smiley's *A Covenant with
Black America* with great interest. I found much to applaud
and agree with in those pages. Yet I was struck by his
glaring omission of the Author of the covenant Himself. Is it
possible to expect a covenant to be honored without honoring
the covenant-keeper? The very foundation for positive change
in any community is the mercy, grace, and sovereign power of

God working through His ambassador and agent of change—
the church.

I recognized that in many ways the church has become
the proverbial ostrich with its head in the sand, thinking that
the problems of our generation no longer exist if we can't see
them. Perhaps this is why the few leaders who appear honestly
concerned with the black community's progress seem content
to ignore the role of the church.

Yet I can't help but wonder if we will see any improvement
in our families without the spiritual and moral discipline
found in the Word of God. Will our communities really grow
stronger without the church as the backbone it once was?
Don't all our fatherless young men still need pastors and spiritual fathers to call them back to wholeness?

I want to begin to briefly address some of the practical
areas where the black community is facing problems today.
We must remember that God's covenant requires something
of both parties. I want to focus on *our* responsibilities to keep
God's covenant in each of these areas.

One of the most important revelations you can ever have in
this lifetime is the understanding of the blessings and benefits
of God's covenant with man. In an era of divorce for "irrecon-
cilable differences," fraud in the business world, and all kinds
of corruption in the political world, we must remember that
our God will keep His covenant. We must also remember that
He expects us to do the same.

> All the ways of the LORD are loving and faithful
> for those who keep the demands of his covenant.
> —Psalm 25:10, NIV

I believe this is absolutely central to the restoration of African-American men and their families. While I welcome the discussion of ways to improve the economic situation for the many African-Americans facing poverty, we are only deceiving ourselves if we think that we can achieve lasting success apart from keeping our covenant with God almighty. How can we restore God's creation without acknowledging the Creator?

> Unless the LORD builds the house, its builders labor in vain. Unless the LORD watches over the city, the watchmen stand guard in vain.
>
> —Psalm 127:1

At the same time the Lord offers a promise:

> If my people, who are called by My name would humble themselves and pray and seek my face and turn from their wicked ways, then will I hear from heaven and will forgive their sin and will heal their land.
>
> —2 Chronicles 7:14

Surely this healing is what we need!

GOD'S FAITHFULNESS TO JOSEPH

When we truly understand the nature of God's covenant, we realize that once God has decided to bless someone, it is impossible for man to thwart His plans. Consider the story of Joseph, sold into slavery by his jealous brothers:

Now Joseph had been taken down to Egypt. And Potiphar, an officer of Pharaoh, captain of the guard, an Egyptian, bought him from the Ishmaelites who had taken him down there. The Lord was with Joseph, and he was a successful man; and he was in the house of his master the Egyptian. And his master saw that the Lord was with him and that the Lord made all he did to prosper in his hand. So Joseph found favor in his sight, and served him. Then he made him overseer of his house, and all that he had he put under his authority. So it was, from the time that he had made him overseer of his house and all that he had, that the Lord blessed the Egyptian's house for Joseph's sake; and the blessing of the Lord was on all that he had in the house and in the field. Thus he left all that he had in Joseph's hand, and he did not know what he had except for the bread which he ate.

—Genesis 39:1–6

Of course most of us remember how it went from there: Potiphar's wife tried to seduce Joseph and when he rebuffed her she lied and landed him in jail yet again. This only paved the way for an even greater promotion, ultimately making Joseph second in command of all Egypt. He summed up his situation perfectly when his brothers came to Egypt seeking food during the drought about which Joseph had warned Pharaoh:

> Joseph said to them, "Do not be afraid, for am I in
> the place of God? But as for you, you meant evil
> against me; but God meant it for good, in order
> to bring it about as it is this day, to save many
> people alive. Now therefore, do not be afraid; I
> will provide for you and your little ones." And he
> comforted them and spoke kindly to them.
>
> —Genesis 50:19–21

It doesn't matter what kinds of trials we face. Joseph proved we can remain faithful through rejection, betrayal, and imprisonment many times over. God will show the same faithfulness to every one of us, if we only keep His covenant.

I realize that there are many experts who debate which set of political policies will create better opportunities for black Americans and ultimately for all Americans. If you listen to one set of politicians, you will come to believe that "Policy X" will solve every problem known to man and that those who oppose "Policy X" are evil beyond belief. If you listen to another set, you may come to believe the same about "Policy Y." That is not what I am primarily concerned with in this book.

Political action is very important, but it has its limitations. No amount of opportunity will help someone who is unwilling or unprepared to take advantage of *any* opportunity. What I want to outline here, in very practical terms, is what families and churches can do right now to address these problems. We do not have to wait until the next election. We do not have to petition our congressmen. These are things we can and MUST do right now.

Healthcare

Proverbs 3:7–8 reminds us, "Do not be wise in your own eyes; fear the LORD and shun evil. This will bring health to your body and nourishment to your bones." Among many other things, heart disease, type two diabetes, and obesity have become major concerns for African-Americans. I commend all the people working to research treatments and cures for these and other diseases. I realize that health insurance and access to medical care are important issues that require a variety of solutions. However, that should not stop us from taking action immediately.

What we can do now:

1. Improve diet and exercise.

There is no reason to wait to start to eat healthier and get more exercise. There may be a thousand different opinions about exactly how to eat, but common sense tells us that a diet rich in fruits and vegetables and whole grains is better than one full of fast food, frozen food, and carryout, which many of us can't afford anyway.

You don't have to join an expensive gym to exercise. Run, walk, or just jump rope at home. Even fifteen minutes a day, if you are completely out of shape, will begin to improve your fitness level a great deal.

Parents must remember that the habits they establish for their children will follow them for the rest of their lives. They must make sure that their children remain active, whether in organized sports for older children or just playing at the park and the pool for younger ones. Children need hours of exercise, not minutes.

Parents should keep healthy snacks like fruit and whole-grain crackers, instead of chips and other junk food. Sodas should be a once-and-a-while treat, not an everyday beverage.

2. Schedule regular exams

You must get regular check-ups and screening for yourself and your children. Too many African-Americans resist going to the doctor for fear of getting bad news. In reality, many conditions and problems are extremely treatable if caught early.

3. Develop and be a part of a healthcare small group.

It can be difficult to change life-long bad habits overnight. Start or join an accountability group for health where you can exchange healthy recipes, encourage each other with exercise goals, and get children together for fitness activities.

Education

There is no question that many of our public schools are failing to educate African-American students. This is a terrible tragedy, especially considering that many of our schools seemed to do a better job during segregation with a lot less money. Even in schools with better records and reputations, too many black students still achieve behind their peers.

Again, there are many opinions about what policy decisions will make our schools better. I want to focus on what every family, community, and church can do to make sure our children are better prepared to take advantage of the all the opportunities they do have.

What we can do now:

1. Read to your children every day.

What if your children spent more time listening to you read to them than watching television or playing video games? Every parent should take time to read not only the Scriptures daily to their children, but also imaginative literature. Create an appetite in your children for the "Great Books" by reading aloud books that are too difficult for them to read by themselves. Many libraries and other educational resources have age-appropriate book lists if you are not sure where to start.

If you are not in the habit of reading to your children, this will take time. Don't give up. Keep trying until you are able to dig into some books that you are all interested in. If your children are preschool age, start with picture books, but move on to more complex stories as their attention spans increase. Encourage your older children to spend time listening to worthwhile audio books in addition to reading and instead of watching television.

2. Volunteer at an after-school program.

Every church that is able to should run an after-school program that provides a safe environment for children to do their homework, play sports, and even receive supplemental teaching in areas like fine arts, dance, and music. To help ensure the children in your community are receiving the best possible encouragement to achieve academically, volunteer at one of these programs, or help to create one.

3. Make your home homework-friendly.

You children will be unable to work effectively if the home is noisy and chaotic. Children of all ages should have an established routine and a clean, quiet space to complete their homework. This can be a desk in their room or it can be at the dining room or kitchen table.

Parents must also check their children's homework daily to ensure that all assignments are complete. They should know, through monitoring their children's work and communicating with the teachers, how their children are performing in every class. If a child is doing poorly in an area, the parent must assess whether he needs tutoring or if privileges should be removed until he works harder. There should be no surprises on that report card.

4. Arrange enriching family and neighborhood activities for children of all ages.

Children do not stumble onto achievement; they are guided and nurtured into it. Why spend eighty dollars taking the kids to see a movie when there are museums that are far cheaper to visit? Don't raise children who are addicted to mindless entertainment. Play educational games and hold community-wide spelling bees and science fairs to supplement what may not be happening effectively at school. Take your children to see the science fairs, orchestra concerts, and academic competitions of older children who are excelling. Take advantage of cultural activities afforded by your locale and budget.

5. Get involved in your children's school.

This may mean joining the PTA or various school committees, volunteering in the classroom, or chaperoning trips. If there is a debate about which math curriculum the school will use next year, you need to know about it. Does the kindergarten use phonics or whole language to teach reading? You should know. Remember, the school is only educating your children because you are delegating your God-given authority to them.

Crime and justice

I have already acknowledged that black men make up a disproportionate percentage of the prison population in the United States. What is often ignored is the fact that the overwhelming majority of these incarcerated men victimized black people with their crimes. They stole from blacks, dealt drugs to blacks, and murdered blacks. Again, there are actions we can all take now that will help ensure that this trend turns around in the next generation.

What we can do now:

1. Teach your children right and wrong.

If you teach your children the Word of God and train them to obey, they will grow up to be responsible citizens. Too many parents think that simply bringing their children to church will accomplish this. That is a start, but it is not enough. As your children grow up, they should not only know that stealing or cheating is wrong, but why it is wrong.

2. Provide children with quality education early.

All the steps outlined above for education will serve as deterrents to your child becoming involved with criminal activity. You must give your child the skills and work ethic he or she needs to be successful outside of the criminal world. They should have enough hope and excitement about their future so that they would never want to risk losing over some friends or other temporary thrills.

3. Provide a reentry program for juvenile ex-offenders.

Churches that are able should create programs to help

ex-offenders of all ages reenter society. This would include spiritual discipleship, vocational training, GED preparation, and counseling. Remember that people with a criminal record can never be allowed unsupervised access to women or children in your church.

Restoring law and order

I have already mentioned the fact that a disproportionate number of black men end up in the prison system. Obviously, no one wants crime to be ignored. We want less crime in the first place. We want young people to conduct themselves honorably. If they find themselves unfairly singled-out for scrutiny, we want them to react with grace and poise. I want to focus on the areas over which we have direct control right now, to improve the black community's relationship with law enforcement.

What can we do now:

1. Get to know the police officers.

Meet the police officers that patrol your neighborhood. Genuine relationships will do much to alleviate and prevent misunderstanding.

2. Host a neighborhood meeting.

Host a neighborhood meeting or ask your local city council representative to host a meeting to discuss local police relations. Sensible discussion can do a lot to offset anger and confusion.

3. Teach young people.

Teach young people how to conduct themselves if they are stopped or confronted by police officers. All young people should be taught proper manners and posture when speaking to any adult, particularly police officers.

4. Establish groups in your local church.

Establish groups in your church for parents whose children are juvenile offenders or deemed "high risk." Ultimately, parents need to intervene as soon as possible to prevent their children from becoming part of the penal system in the first place.

Housing and ownership

We all know it can be tough to get ahead. Living in a bad neighborhood can point some good kids in the wrong direction. Lower income parents are often forced to keep their children inside all the time to avoid the dangers lurking down the block. I recognize that we need a variety of policy solutions to address this complicated situation. There are also, however, things we can do right now to ensure we leave an inheritance to our children's children.

What we can do now:

1. Pray.

Like Nehemiah, we can pray and commit to productive action for our own families and neighborhoods. Improvement starts at home. Have neighborhood clean-up days and encourage your neighbors to take pride in the appearance of their block.

2. Join a self-help housing project.

Join a project such as Habitat for Humanity to build your house or help build someone else's.

3. Give a working car away.

Donate a car to a deserving single parent. Some housing is out of reach to those who have no way to transport themselves to work. A car without the burden of a car loan can help a hard-working mother get ahead.

4. Be involved.

Be involved when decisions are being made for public transportation. Let your voice be heard concerning future plans and developments.

5. Be a homeowner.

For most Americans, their homes will be their single most important asset. If you do not already own your home, make a plan to purchase one in the near future.

6. Find out if your family owns land.

If they do, reach out to other family members to ensure that they hold onto that land.

Responsible citizenship

Our forefathers suffered and died for our right to vote, and yet so many of us do not choose to exercise it. In a democracy it is our responsibility to choose the best leaders we can for every position available. We must vote for policies that reflect the Bible as closely as possible. If we do not, we will have only ourselves to blame when our government does not work the way it should.

What we can do now:

1. Pray and get involved.

Who makes the decisions that affect your immediate neighborhood? You should know the members of the school board, city council, and board of county commissioners, and they should know you.

2. *Register to vote.*

Cast an informed vote in all elections. Make sure before each election that you have thoroughly researched each candidate and any referenda that may be on the ballot.

3. *Teach your children.*

You must educate your children about the importance of participating in the political process by being an informed voter. Your children are much more likely to become responsible citizens if they see your example.

4. *Create advocacy small groups.*

Establish groups to educate the church and community about critical issues in your city.

These are all actions that every one of us can take right now. We don't have to wait for the next election, or the next town council meeting. I believe these kinds of actions are key to strengthening our families, rebuilding our communities, and reestablishing the church as the backbone of our community.

PARTING THOUGHTS

MANY PEOPLE WOULD have us believe that the black community has outgrown its need for the church. They tell us we need programs without God, policy change without spiritual change. I believe they have it backwards. The black community needs God more than ever. Those of us who are foundering in a destructive ghetto culture need Him to rescue us and change our minds and hearts. Those of us who are prospering need Him to remind us about what we have been spared so that we can become part of His solution.

No program will ever change the fact that Dad is destiny. The only hope for healing for those whose fathers have forsaken them is Jesus Christ and His church. Only God can grace us to overcome the multitudes of excuses the enemy will use to blind us to our opportunities. African-American men must discard once and for all the victim mentality that has plagued us for ages.

There is healing and wholeness in the black church. More importantly there is hope for black men—the Hope of Glory, Jesus the Christ, Son of the Living God. It is only through His redeeming blood and grace that men of any color can reclaim what God gave Adam in the Garden—a plan and purpose for living, nurturing, and multiplying. As men begin to follow this plan, they will take charge of the spiritual upbringing of the next generation, especially during the transition period from childhood to adolescence, when they are most likely to lose their way. These men will heed the African proverb that reminds us to *bend the tree while it is green.*

I believe if we can make our churches more welcoming to black men and seek them out more aggressively, we will see the tide turn. I truly believe that Jesus is the answer; just as men carried the sick to Jesus to heal, we must go into the neighborhoods and streets and bring African-American men to Jesus. I believe this will not only revive and restore the black community, but also the nation as a whole.

It is my sincerest desire that African-American men today would return to the church, find their rightful place, and fulfill the every hope and desire that God has for them. The time is coming when men will once again rise early to warm up the car on those cold winter Sundays. Fathers will show their sons how to tie a tie before service, and help their daughters up the steps into the sanctuary. No mother will sit in a pew without her husband's arm around her shoulder. And God will see from heaven and smile.

APPENDIX

Questionnaire Responses From Three African-American Pastors Who Have Successfully Created Cultures in the Church Conducive to Black Men

Apostle Otis Lockett, Sr.

Apostle Otis Lockett, Sr., is senior pastor of three thousand-member Evangel Fellowship Church in Greensboro, NC. Evangel Fellowship Church has been widely respected and considered a leader in the church world for its profound effects toward reaching and discipling African-American men. He is also chairman of the National Church Growth and Development Department for the Church of God in Christ worldwide.

Q: What are the biggest challenges facing African-American men in America today?

A: Purpose and having a sense of destiny; racism; economics/financial; family

Q: What has the church neglected most in the lives of African-American men today?

A: Understanding the unique challenges of being African-American

Q: What is uniquely different about your leadership and personal influence as it directly relates to the discipling of African-American men?

A: I intentionally seek to make the gospel of Christ relevant to their total needs.

Q: What is particularly different about the culture and environment of the church you pastor as it relates to strengthening and supporting African-American men?

A: We honor and challenge men to be the best they can be for God in every area of their lives.

Q: What should the church today do to help create a climate and culture conducive for African-American men?

A: Provide men with services that address their total needs: (a) mentoring young boys; (b) men's groups to discuss challenging issues; (c) train them for leadership in and out of the church arena; (d) preach and teach the Bible as it relates to their unique needs.

Pastor Cliff Lovick

Pastor Cliff Lovick is senior pastor of Recovery Christian Center in Asheboro, North Carolina, and executive director of the Malachi House, a twelve-month residential mentoring program designed to assist men who are struggling with life-controlling problems such as drug and alcohol addiction.

Q: What are the biggest challenges facing African-American men (AA) in America today?

A: One of the challenges for AA is that we are still victims of racism. Also the socioeconomic status in America tends to exclude the AA when it comes to abundance, which has created poverty. We seem to have constant struggle. Many

AA live a life of low self-esteem and lack of confidence, which affects the whole family.

Q: What has the church neglected most in the lives of African-American men today?

A: Most churches lack the ability to create empowerment strategies because they don't understand the black culture, and that is a crucial role in fostering development. For example, a great percentage of AA men were raised without a father in the home, so the need for a spiritual dad is a must. Mentoring is another crucial element for building relationship. Sometimes in church we talk at people and not to the heart of the matter. It will require the church to get a new perspective on male empowerment, which will include language, style, authenticity, and spiritual counseling.

Q: What is uniquely different about your leadership and personal influence as it directly relates to the discipling of African-American men?

A: John Maxwell said that before you ask for someone's hand you must cultivate a relationship with their hearts. People are not concerned with how much you know. They are concerned with how much you care. Rule without relationship creates rebellion. I really believe that the men at the Malachi House, which is a twelve-month faith-based drug rehab, follow my leadership because they know I care deeply for them.

Q: What is particularly different about the culture and environment of the church you pastor as it relates to strengthening and supporting African-American men?

A: In order for your church to become conducive and create a culture for the AA, study the needs of your particular men and begin to assimilate classes that will develop. For example: fathering classes, business classes, finance classes, or educational classes.

Dr. Patrick L. Wooden

Dr. Patrick L. Wooden is senior pastor of the 2,500-member Upper Room Church of God in Christ in Raleigh, North Carolina. He is the recipient of numerous awards, including Religious Leader of the Year and Humanitarian of the Year. He has been featured in several media outlets including CNN, ABC, CBS, NBC, *The O'Reilly Factor*, and a host of national radio stations. He is best known for being a builder of strong men and boldly preaching about issues that affect today's society as he lives by the principle of *keeping God first*!

Q: What are the biggest challenges facing African-American men in America today?

A: Failure to adhere to the Christian doctrine. The main reason for failure to adhere to the Christian doctrine is because it is no longer taught in most churches in America today. There is the prosperity doctrine, word of faith doctrine (Black Liberation theology), Osteenism, Oprahism, Jakesism, and the like. But all of these "isms" combined are not the Christian doctrine.

Paul warned that the day would come when men would not listen to sound doctrine. We are still, however, commanded to "preach the Word" (2 Tim. 4:2). As ministers of the gospel, we are to be "nourished in the words of faith, and of good doctrine" (1 Tim. 4:6).

Q: What has the church neglected most in the lives of African-American men today?

A: Expository preaching of the gospel of Christ. African-American men in many ways don't know who they are and what their purpose is. Many pastors have adopted the motivational speakers' style of delivery and have incorporated other doctrines and disciplines and human sciences to address these and other similar questions. Expository preaching and teaching is the key. Proclaiming and explaining the Word of God is the answer.

Knowing God's Word is the key to fulfillment in this life and the life to come, period! Paul says to Timothy, "Til I come give attendance to...doctrine" (1 Tim. 4:13). Also, the sixteenth verse of this same chapter says, "Take heed unto thyself, and unto the doctrine."

Q: What is uniquely different about your leadership and personal influence as it directly relates to the discipling of African-American men?

A: Expository preaching. The Word of God is for everyone. The greatest stories ever told are in the Bible. Nothing speaks to the man or the male, African-American or otherwise, like the line-upon-line preaching and teaching of the Word of God. God's Word kept Israel and saw them through when they were minorities in Babylon. God's Word blessed Daniel when he was a minority in Babylon. He and his friends climbed the social ladder of success without eating the king's meat! I teach men who they are through the Word of God, not through humanism or secular psychology, not through endless sessions of pastoral counseling, but through the guise of Psalm 1:1–2, "Blessed is the man that walketh not in the counsel of the ungodly, nor standeth in the way of sinners, nor sitteth in the seat of the scornful. But his delight is in the law of the LORD; and in his law doth he meditate day and night."

Q: What is particularly different about the culture and environment of the church you pastor as it relates to strengthening and supporting African-American men?

A: The African-American male has been attacked from every side. From Willie Lynch to self-inflected words that we have to remind us of how great we are and how wonderful our culture is. Again, the Christian doctrine addresses these things. In Acts 15 we learn that we don't have to give up our culture and become white people or anyone else to serve the Lord. There are some destructive aspects of our culture (as with all others) that we need to attack and get rid of. For instance, Hip Hop, the glorification of the destruction of the black community; an entire industry of music that is dedicated to the denigration of America's most beautiful women. The look, the sound, the manner, the way of Hip Hop is the way of death for African-Americans. We must address these issues. Sexual immorality and perversion is a major cultural challenge to us. Again the Christian doctrine addresses these things. The prophet Isaiah says in Isaiah 55:6–7, "Seek ye the LORD while he may be found, call ye upon him while he is near: and the wicked forsake his way, and the unrighteous man his thoughts: and let him return unto the LORD, and he will have mercy upon him; and to our God, for he will abundantly pardon."

Q: What should the church today do to help create a climate and culture conducive for African-American men?

A: The church should raise the bar of expectation on African-American men with love and consideration. Historically, the African-American male has been a symbol of strength and might. The black man stood strong through Jim Crow, the Klan, and a government that would send him to war, but would not allow him to vote. He stood strong through humiliation and segregation, all the while believing in the God of Moses and "we shall overcome someday." Today he is soft, dumbed-down, and a victim of low expectations. The word of the prophet Jeremiah comes to mind: "Let them return unto thee, but return not unto them" (Jer. 5:19).

That is, raise the bar. The black man is a great man; all immigrants who have come to this country since the sixties owe a debt of thanks to the African-American male and female for that matter. The way to, "create the climate that is conducive" for us is to remind us that our Lord said, "Without me you can do nothing" (John 15:5), and that Paul said, "I can do all things through Christ" (Phil. 4:13).

ABOUT THE AUTHOR

MICHAEL A. STEVENS, Sr., is a man of God who passionately pursues the promises of the Father in heaven concerning life, success, and faithfulness. It was in 1994 that Pastor Stevens founded University City Church. Beginning with only two members, this life-changing and impacting ministry now exceeds 1,100 members in just over thirteen years of ministry. Pastor Stevens is also an ordained elder and district superintendent in the Church of God in Christ.

He is a 1992 graduate of North Carolina A & T State University, located in Greensboro, North Carolina, where he earned a Bachelor of Science degree in political studies. He recently graduated with his Master's of Divinity degree from Oral Roberts University and is currently enrolled in the Doctorate of Ministry program.

Charisma magazine in 2005 named Pastor Stevens one of Thirty Emerging Voices under the age of forty for this next generation of church leadership. Pastor Stevens has been privileged to preach coast-to-coast and abroad in such countries as South Africa, Peru, Bermuda, Kenya, Belize, and Israel.

Pastor Stevens is also host of *The Michael A. Stevens Show* on NewsTalk 1110, WBT, on the AM dial, and *On the Mic with Pastor Mike* on Praise 100.9 FM, Charlotte's inspiration station.

Pastor Stevens is the author of the book *Straight Up: The*

Church's Official Response to the Epidemic of Down-Low Living, published by Creation House in 2006, and was the subject of a feature interview in the June 2006 *Charisma* magazine.

Pastor Michael is married to his college sweetheart, Sharon, and together they have been blessed with three children, Michael, Jr., Matthew Courtlin, and Charisma Lindsey.

To Contact the Author

www.michaelastevens.com

NOTES

INTRODUCTION

1. John W. Fountain, "No Place for Me: I Still Love God, But I've Lost Faith in the Black Church," *The Washington Post,* July 17, 2005.

2. Bill Hybels, *Courageous Leadership* (Grand Rapids, MI: Zondervan, 2002).

3. Quote available at http://Kinetics.squarespace .com/brother/, accessed May 23, 2008.

CHAPTER 1
FROM INVINCIBLE TO INVISIBLE

1. Ralph Ellison, *The Invisible Man* (New York: Vintage, 1995).

2. "The Compromise Speech," September 1, 1895 in Atlanta, Georgia, www.usa-patriotism.com/ speeches, accessed May 23, 2008.

3. Quote available at http://www.washingtonpost .com/wpdyn/content/article/2006/10/07/ AR2006100701070.html, accessed May 23, 2008.

4. Quote available at http://www.jointcenter.org/DB/ factsheet/marital.htm, accessed May 23, 2008.

5. Quote available at http://www.jointcenter.org/DB/ factsheet/marital.htm, accessed May 23, 2008.

6. Michael Stevens, *Straight Up: The Church's Official Response to the Epidemic of Down-Low Living* (Lake Mary, FL: Creation House, 2005).

7. "Black Men and Church," blog site accessed September 8, 2006, http://daneger06.blogspot.com/2006/09/black-men-and-church-long-article.html.

8. Ibid.

CHAPTER 2
IN THE BEGINNING

1. Quote available at http://www.mlkonline.net/quotes.html, accessed June 4, 2008.

2. Barna Research Group, Ltd. Barna.Org, Flex Page Gender Differences, 2007.

CHAPTER 3
FATHERLESS FATHERS

1. Joseph P. Shapiro, Joannie M. Schrof, Mike Tharp, and Dorian Friedman, "Honor Thy Children," *U.S. News and World Report*, Feb. 27, 1995.

2. Jeanne Machado and Helen Meyer-Botnarescue, *Student Teaching: Early Childhood Practicum Guide* (n.p.: Thomson Delmar Learning, 2004), 374.

3. Shapiro, "Honor Thy Children."

4. Discussion between Dr. Larry K King and Dr. James Dobson on the subject of homosexuality, November 22, 2006; The Larry King Show on CNN.

5. Fagan, Patrick F., *The Heritage Foundation*, "Why Religion Matters: The Impact of Religious Practice on Social Stability," January 25, 1996.

6. Ibid.

7. Ibid.

8. Ibid.

CHAPTER 4
FINDING THE FATHER

1. Terry Tempest Williams, *Red: Passion and Patience in the Desert* (New York: Pantheon, 2001).

CHAPTER 5
WHY WE STILL NEED THE CHURCH

1. "On the Unity of the Catholic Church," www.romancatholicism.org.

2. Fagan, *Why Religion Matters.*

3. Fagan, Patrick F. *The Heritage Foundation Backgrounder*, "Why Religion Matters: The Impact of Religious Practice on Social Stability," January 25, 1996.

4. Leanne Payne, *Crisis in Masculinity* (Grand Rapids, MI: Baker Books, 1995).

5. Ibid., 11.

6. Ibid., 12.

7. Stevens, *Straight Up: The Church's Official Response to the Epidemic of Down-Low Living.*

Chapter 6
Turning the Tide

1. David Murrow, *Why Men Hate Going to Church*. (Nashville: Thomas Nelson, 2005), 7.

2. Ibid.

3. Dr. Jawanza Kunjufu, *Adam! Where Are You?: Why Most Black Men Don't Go to Church* (Sauk Village, IL: African American Images, 1997).

4. Fagan, "Why Religion Matters."

Chapter 7
Creating a Culture

1. George Barna, *Growing True Disciples* (Colorado Springs: WaterBrook Press, 2001).

2. Williams, *Red: Passion and Patience in the Desert*.

3. Murrow, *Why Men Hate Going to Church*.

Chapter 8
Renewing the Covenant

1. West India Emancipation Speech, Aug. 4, 1857, "If there is no struggle, there is no progress," www.blackpast.com, accessed May 23, 2008.